S.O.L

20 Shades of Love | 16 Shades of Lunar | XII Staves of Lore

Anogh Roy Acharya

BookLeaf Publishing
India | USA | UK

Made with ❤ on the BookLeaf Publishing Platform
www.bookleafpub.in
www.bookleafpub.com

Dedication

SOL is not a singular journey; it unfolds as a three part sensory experience that explores love, time, and transformation.

20 Shades of Love invites you into a gallery of emotions, where love, loss, and longing are frozen in vivid imagery. Each poem is a photograph, each word a color, offering an experience to see and feel the weight of untamed emotions.

16 Shades of Lunar shifts to sound, weaving stories through the moon's phases and melodies. It does not just speak—it sings, resonating with violins, crashing waves, and whispered emotions, creating an auditory odyssey.

XII Staves of Lore is a hymn to time, where each month becomes a poetic guide. Like a SOLar calendar, it reflects on life's cycles, transitions, and the rhythm of endings becoming beginnings.

Dedication

To The Ones Who Seek

To The Ones Who Read
To The Ones Who Heal
To The Ones Who Believe

To the times being lived (Aekaal)
To the times gone by (Shekaal)

And To the late Dr. Raichand

PREFACE

"Hi," came a mortifying male voice that vibrated in my eardrums. Every time this guy says hello, these days, I feel an unsettling pity for myself.

"Ne okay, ano (Are you okay) ? Mayank?" Anjali's voice cut in, the concern in her tone unmistakable, softened by the Thrissur lilt of her Malayalam. Mayank, standing awkwardly, took a deep breath, as though summoning whatever was left of his willpower. Then, with a dramatic surrender to gravity, he collapsed into a dark blue bean bag thrown carelessly on the floor.

Our muscle memory jolted Anjali and me into action, but seeing that Mayank had landed safely, we relaxed. We moved toward him and sat nearby, a comfortable silence settling over the room. He stared at the black dreamcatcher hanging from the ceiling, lost in thought. While freezing himself in the same position, stretching the membrane of his throat, he moved his Adam's apple and uttered, "I just feel like someone reached down my throat, grabbed my small intestine, pulled it out of my mouth, and tied it around my neck…"

Okay, okay, okay! I know what you're thinking—yes, it sounds suspiciously like something Ross Geller would say. Honestly, the whole scene feels like a knockoff of FRIENDS—with me and Anjali awkwardly standing in as Joey and Monica. But here's the thing: Mayank's heartbreak carries the same weight as Ross's first-episode blues. His sulking, "I-can't-catch-a-break" face? Absolutely genuine. He was drowning in the kind of heartbreak that makes even cheesy lines sound poetic.

Somewhere in the back of my mind, I imagined Zubin's sarcastic quip echoing in response to Mayank's misery. He'd probably say something like, "Only you could make intestinal knots sound like Shakespeare, dude." And Rahul? He'd likely offer a philosophical ramble about how pain and love are just cosmic dances that repeat themselves across lifetimes.

But neither Zubin's wit nor Rahul's cosmic musings could change the fact that Mayank was spiraling after the end of his relationship with Sindhu. Yes, the Sindhu from my previous book, 20 Shades of Love. They broke up, despite the book suggesting otherwise. Turns out, real life doesn't follow neat, happy endings. But honestly, I was kind of hoping that my book would fix their love story. I mean, it's one thing to write about love, but it's another to think that maybe—just maybe—my words could rewrite

reality.
Spoiler: they did not.

20 Shades of Love was released on September 13, 2022—a date that, coincidentally, is also the birthday of one of the book's first editors, **Vasabdatta Sen**. I thought the story was done. Mayank's story had found its audience—the book traveled to Pragati Maidan's Delhi Book Fair in 2024, made an appearance at the KV Cossipore Alumni Meet in 2023, and even popped up at a café in Bhubaneswar (shout-out to **Abhishek Sahu** for that unexpected update) While we are at it, a random shout out to **Dhruv Khanna**. But as much as the story traveled, it didn't solve anything. Because love is not something you solve—it is a cycle you survive.

And so, here we are again. Another story. Another set of emotions. Another moon phase to navigate. This time, the story will unfold across 8 phases of the lunar cycle—from the new moon to the full moon—each told from two perspectives. That makes 16 entries. Why? Because the moon has its phases, just like life. And sometimes, what looks like an ending is just the start of something new.

And why dual perspectives? Because I can not stop Mayank from jumping into these white pages. He can emerge any freaking mo…

Hi! I'm Mayank. Sorry for interrupting. Remember me? From 20 Shades of Love—or #20SOL, as Mr. A insists on calling it. In case you haven't read it, I recommend you start with it (find it in this book).

No? Not convinced? Okay, as you wish.

Honestly, I think Mr. A is addicted to acronyms. And now, here we are with another one—#16SOL. Typical Mr. A and his endless wordplay obsession.

Let's address the elephant in the room: the title of this book is 16 Shades of Lunar, yet there are 21 entries. Why? Because Mr. A has an inexplicable knack for overcomplicating things. Don't even ask why he threw in five extra chapters. Apparently, the phases of the moon weren't enough—he had to toss in asteroids and rare celestial events for good measure. Classic Mr. A.

Anyway, I'm Mayank Agarwal. I come from Manipal, the student town on the southern coast of Karnataka. To some, it's just a place; to those who've lived there, it's a phenomenon. You don't choose Manipal; it chooses you. Take a student out of Manipal, but you'll never get the Manipalite spirit out of them. It's like the Red Sofa from Friends' fictional Central Perk—you just keep circling back.

Now, back to the Preface. As far as I can tell, the following pages will break my life—and maybe Mr. A's too—into 16 shades. Each shade mirrors a phase of the moon, waxing and waning, just like life. So why dual perspectives? Because Mr. A can't seem to resist dragging me back into these white pages. He's got this annoying knack for inserting me wherever he wants. I'm not even sure if it's still my story or if I've just become a character in his chaotic narrative experiments.

Before you dive in, there's one more thing. Each chapter comes with a suggested audio track to enhance your reading experience. Play it on loop for the best effect. Mr. A insists it sets the "perfect vibe." I'm not sure if it does, but I'll let you decide. Please, go ahead—I insist too.

We'll find out together what lies ahead. Either way, the moon keeps waxing and waning, and the show must go on.

16 Shades of Lunar

Anogh Roy Acharya

Acknowledgements

Dear Co-Orbiters,

In this cosmic journey of life, we are all in orbit—moving through phases, pulling each other's gravity, and influencing one another's path, much like the moon. You, my readers, are my Co-Orbiters—sharing this story's trajectory, whether you joined by chance or by choice.

I convey my Eightfold Regards—
Genuine, Warm, Kind, Respectful, Fond, Sincere, Faithful, and Best Regards—
as a reflection of the many ways gratitude can manifest, just as the moon reflects its light in various phases.

To whoever, wherever, however, happens to grab (literally & metaphorically) this tiny book,
And eventually read ; **To you**, my dear readers.

To
Rahul & Anjali (ഞാൻ നിങ്ങളെ കണ്ടെത്തിയ ഒരു പാത തിരഞ്ഞെടുത്തതിന് നന്ദി)
Prateem & Piyali (Growing up with them has been truly amazing)
Heartfulness & Daaji (The exploration is interesting)

To the Loudest Cheerers & Silent Supporters.
Srijita (বাইদেউ), Didreekshmaa (Dyuti), and Debolina (Guddi),
To the four-legged loves—Phoebe and Bluebo.

To #EPRPublicSchool ; Boss Man: Santhanam Srinivasan Iyer.

To the ones making Manipal 2.0 bearable: They know who they are

To
Mi Familia! Roys & Acharyas.
Special Thanks to Mrs. Shubhalakshmi, আমার দিম্মি, for the name that she bestowed upon me.

With Love,
Chaand (My Pet Name | Aamar Daak Naam)

1. New Moon: The First Breath of Emptiness

To be paired with: ♪ **Pause** – Prateek Kuhad
Category: **Letter**

Mayank feels like everything has hit a reset button—his love is gone, and the world feels weightless but eerily empty. It's a moment where nothingness reigns, and emotions are muted. What is going on, inside Mayank's head?

The First Breath of Emptiness

A room full of things, yet ***hollow*** *with* ***silence****.*
Gravity *pulls, but not with the same force anymore.*
I lie here, not falling—just ***floating in place****.*
The ***moon*** *hides itself tonight, and so do I.*

The clock ticks, but each second slips into an ***endless void****.*
No ***echoes****, no* ***meaning****—just sound that* ***fades*** *mid-air.*
The ***dreamcatcher*** *sways above my head, catching only memories.*
They ***tangle****, slip through its web, and disappear,*
Just like she lied—without warning, without staying to

explain.

Is this what ***nothingness*** *feels like?*
Not sharp like pain, not heavy like sorrow—
But a ***quiet blur****, where* ***emotions flicker***
And ***dim out*** *before they can ignite.*

I lie on this ***beanbag****, the weight of my body*
Pressing down, but my ***heart—light as smoke****.*
Uncertain if it drifts upward, or dissolves right here.
This room has walls, but tonight it feels ***borderless****,*
Like a ***sky without stars****, a* ***sea without shorelines****.*
They say the ***new moon*** *marks a beginning,*
But how do you start something
When everything that ***tethered*** *you has* ***unraveled****?*
This ***darkness*** *isn't peace—it's an* ***empty space****,*
A ***waiting room*** *between* ***endings*** *and* ***beginnings****.*
I ***exhale****.*

The air feels ***foreign*** *in my lungs.*
As if I'm ***borrowing breath*** *from a world*
I no longer recognize.
Still, in the ***void****, there is a hint—*
That maybe, just maybe,
This ***emptiness*** *is the* ***soil*** *where something* ***new*** *might grow.*
Not today.

Maybe not tomorrow.
*But **One Day**.*
***Someday**.*

Pheweep.
A sudden notification sound yanks my attention back to my phone. It's a text from Rahul, of course. That guy has a knack for showing up right when the silence gets too loud.

"Bro? Should we go to the beach tonight?"
Rahul's energy is always offbeat, floating somewhere between chaotic wisdom and pure randomness—the kind that makes him the Phoebe Buffay of our lives. One moment, he'll say something absurd like, "The moon doesn't show up every night because it needs alone time too," and the next, he'll drop a piece of wisdom so profound you can't stop thinking about it for days.

I show the message to Anjali, her eyes lighting up instantly. But after a moment of hesitation, she frowns.
"But it's Amavasya today," she says, twisting the nose ring on her right nostril thoughtfully. "So, not good moon today or tomorrow." She pauses for a beat and then adds, "Umm... Can we go see

the sunset? Pleassee, Plllleeaasseee, Pleaacchhhe!" She said it exactly in the spelt accent.

Sunset at the beach is indeed a visual treat, especially here on the western coast of India. But there's something magical about walking along the moonlit shore—the way the water glows under the night sky, as if the ocean has borrowed light from the stars.

Ignoring the sunset plan, I pitch my own idea. "Can we go on a Purnima (Full Moon) night instead?"
Anjali's face softens into a smile as she tucks a stray curl behind her ear. "Yes," she says with a grin. "We can do that someday."

And just like that, the weight in the room lifts, if only a little. The mention of the beach, sunsets, and moonlit nights gives us something to look forward to. Someday, I think. Maybe, just maybe, that thought will be enough, for tonight.

2. New Moon: Side B

To be paired with: ♪ **Pause** – Prateek Kuhad
Category: **Letter**

We were at the ***beach****. Rahul had dragged me along with* ***Mr. A****,* ***Anjali****, and* ***Zubin****. The* ***salty breeze*** *mixed with the* ***rhythmic crashing****of waves, the perfect soundtrack for one of those* ***moonless****, in-between nights. Zubin had flown in from* ***Mumbai****, with a shaved head, needing a break from the endless grind of his film career. While Rahul had taken his art-film ambitions back to* ***Kerala****, Zubin from* ***Ranchi****was still chasing* ***Mumbai's chaos****, trying to find humor in a city that didn't slow down. They were the kind of friends who met in* ***Manipal****during their bachelor's and stayed close, no matter where life took them.*

If ***Rahul*** *was the* ***Phoebe Buffay*** *of the group—random and spiritual—****Zubin*** *was definitely our* ***Chandler Bing****. He had a sarcastic comment for everything, wearing his* ***humor like armor*** *to fend off anything serious. If someone said, "I'm having an* ***existential crisis****," Zubin would deadpan, "Try turning it off and on again."*

Tonight, though, even Zubin had gone quiet, content to

sit and listen to the ***waves****, as if the* ***sea*** *had more jokes than he did.*

Somewhere between these moments of ***silence****, I found myself walking beside* ***Mr. A****. He seemed unusually* ***lost****, even for someone who thinks too much. After a while, he sighed and turned to me.*

"I want to show you something," he said, pulling out his phone. "A letter I wrote... exactly standing here, after witnessing a sunset, three years ago."
I saw the heading and uttered softly, "You read it out, Macha!"

He obeyed.

Mr. A's Letter to an Unknown Address

September 3rd 2021

Dear Amma,
It's been more than a year since you left us, and somehow the weight of that absence feels heavier, not lighter. 2020 was difficult—for me and for so many others. I lost friends, made new ones. I smiled when I wanted to cry. I tried to stand tall, and then I fell again.

But your absence was the hardest.
Some lost a mother, others lost a teacher, a sister, or a guide. But you were more than all of that for me—you were my solace.
The first day of last year began with your loss. You were the first teacher I ever had, even though I wasn't the most attentive student but " আমি তোমার জন্য যেটুকু হোক বাংলা লিখতে ও পড়তে জানি" (How much ever I know how to read and write Bangla, it is for you only)."
Since then, not only us but the entire world has been in distress. Obviously, they should have known. How can a year be good, if it starts with the loss of a noble soul like yours?

I have failed many times, in the past year. I have fallen down and have fallen deep. But I have remembered your words. I have stood up after every punch, after every hit; every kick. Once you had said, *"Sometime, floating is enough. No need to struggle against the current by trying to swim."* So, I am doing the same. I am hanging in there. Your blessings are my strength and soon, I will start swimming and I will swim fast.
Just like me, the world has changed a lot too. It has seen the best of humanity and the worst of humanity. It has seen lynching; it has seen support for farming. It has seen hatred towards love, it has seen love; well, that is enough. However, you have taught me to see the world,

as the beauty it is. I have seen sunrises and sunsets. I have seen waterfalls, clouds, and beaches. I am falling in love with this world and the mankind; irrespective of what it becomes. I will preach your teachings to whoever is in need. I will educate the wrongdoers with my last drop of energy. I will try to be happy and will try to make this world a kinder place; that accepts all. I shall and I will.

Today, I saw a sunset that reminded me of you.

The sky burned with red and gold as the sun sank into the ocean. And in that moment, I realized something: I'm not afraid of darkness anymore. Because now I know that after every night, the sun will rise again—just like you taught me to rise after every fall.

Wherever you are, Amma, I hope you've found peace. You gave enough of yourself to this world. Now, it's time for you to rest.

Lots of Love.
Yours Forever,
A.

I glanced at ***Mr. A*** *as he finished reading the* ***letter*** *aloud. The evening sky had started to dim, the* ***orange hues*** *melting into softer* ***blues****, and the* ***waves*** *rolled in, soft and steady, as if they knew we needed the* ***space*** *to absorb everything he'd just shared.*

For a moment, the only sounds were the **waves** *and the distant chatter of kids playing down the shore.* **Rahul***,* **Zubin***, and* **Anjali** *sat a little distance away, lost in their own thoughts. Even* **Zubin***—our resident* **sarcastic genius***—was unusually quiet, staring out at the* **horizon** *like the* **ocean** *had stolen his punchlines.*

I nudged him. "What's up, **Chandler***? No punchline this time?"*
He smirked, but only a little. "This whole thing's too **Guchhipudi***, man."*

I blinked. "What does that even mean?"
He shrugged. "A full-on disaster, with a side of unnecessary drama. Like a bad **soap opera** *where everyone forgot their lines and just started* **crying***."*
I laughed. There he was—our **Zubin***. Even in the heavy moments, he had a way of making things* **lighter** *without dismissing them.*

Rahul *leaned back, propping himself on his elbows. "You know what I think? This* **beach** *and us? Feels like... a* **film***, bro."*
I rolled my eyes. "Of course it does. You've been directing our lives since day one. First, why don't you

release that long-awaited film of yours—'Fiction'?"
***Rahul** grinned, not the least bit offended. "That will happen in its own time, bro. I know that it's been five years since graduation. But great **art** takes time."*
*"Yeah, yeah," **Zubin** muttered. "By the time 'Fiction' comes out, it'll be a **period film** about **millennials** dealing with midlife crises."*
***Rahul** grinned. "**Common Man**! Let's focus here. I see potential in this **cast**."*
***Anjali** chuckled, adjusting her **nose ring**. "I'll play myself."*
***Rahul** pointed dramatically at her.*
*"Brilliant. **Zubin's** obviously **Chandler**. **Mayank** is **Ross**, sulking over his breakup. And that leaves..."*
*He swung his arm towards **Mr. A**, who looked like he wanted to dissolve into the **sand**. "**Monica**! Meticulous, well-spoken, and always holding us together."*
*Raising one hand in protest, **A** shook his head. "No way. I'm not **Monica**. I'd rather be **Joey**."*
*"Yeah, no," **Zubin** shot back with a grin. "If you're **Joey**, we're already **Guchhipudi-level doomed**."*
*The whole group broke into **laughter**, the kind that catches you off guard and leaves you a little **breathless**. When the laughter finally subsided, the **silence** that followed felt **lighter**, more **bearable**—like we'd let out a breath we didn't know we were holding.*

*I turned to **Mr. A**, watching as the last streaks of **daylight** dissolved into the **sea**.*
*"When did you write that **letter**?"*
*He stared at the **waves**, his expression **soft** but **distant**.*
"Before I met you."
*"Right before you stopped **swimming**?" I asked quietly.*
*He smiled, but it was **small** and **tired**. "Yeah. That night, I just... stopped."*

*We let the **silence** stretch between us again, the **waves** lapping gently at the **shore**. For a while, it was enough to just stand there, **side by side**, without saying anything.*
*And then—because of course it had to be **Rahul**—he broke the silence with a grin.*
"Ice cream, anyone?"
***Zubin** groaned. "It's not even **dark** yet, man."*
*"And?" **Rahul** shot back, already brushing the **sand** off his jeans.*
***Anjali** stood up, smiling. "I'm in!"*
*I shook my head but found myself **grinning** anyway.*

*This was us. Floating through life, one **random**, ridiculous decision at a time. **Ice cream** with a tonsil, on an **Amavasya** (New Moon) evening? Sure, why not?*

As we walked towards the distant glow of

the ***streetlights****, I thought about what* ***Mr. A*** *had said—about stopping and floating. Maybe that's what we were doing tonight—floating together, trusting the* ***tide*** *to take us wherever it wanted.*

And for now? That felt like enough.

I can finally ***breathe****; no need to* ***chase*** *or resist.*

3. Waxing Crescent: Hiding Today

To be paired with: ♪ **Hiding Tonight** - Alex Turner

Category: **Letter**

Mayank has been... restless. I see it in the way his foot taps against the chair leg, like he's trying to find a rhythm that won't come. He checks his phone too often, scrolling without really reading—waiting for something that isn't there. Mayank is the kind of person who doesn't dive back into life with a splash—he wades in, cautiously, testing the waters.

That's where Zubin comes in, flying in like a half-baked angel. He is not a life coach by any means—more like an accidental philosopher with a knack for sarcasm. Today, Zubin summoned us to Manipal Residency, holed up in his Bat-cave on the first floor with an iMac churning out Premiere Pro renders, while he justifies his ridiculous obsession with Big Macs—'two Macs, one soul,' as he calls it. He even insisted we go eat at **MacD** to cut down on takeaway **wrappers** polluting the environment, but I declined—I've got enough papers to wrestle with today.

I'm in a sunlit corner, half-listening to their banter while working on my conference abstract. Kudos to my supervisor's last-minute mail.

Meanwhile, Mayank stares at Zubin's screenplay pages, his curiosity piqued.

"What's with all the **scattered pages**?" he asks, poking at them like they might bite. Zubin leans back, his sunglasses glinting in the soft afternoon light. "It's a vignette script—just fragments of scenes. No full story, just glimpses."

I scan through academic citations on my laptop, the task of condensing an idea into 300 words weighing on my mind. It's a delicate thing, writing an abstract. Like a summary of a story that hasn't been told yet.

A story that has not been told yet.

*The **air** is **warm**, and **sunlight** filters through **Zubin's window**, casting **pale gold patches** on the **floor**. The **smell** of **fries** and **stale coffee** hangs in the **room**, mingling with the **faint hum** of his **iMac**. **Zubin's room** is **chaotic**, **cluttered** with **scripts**, **wires**, and a **second-hand camera**, but it feels... **safe**, in an odd way.*

***Zubin** leans back in his **chair**, spinning it **lazily**, the **afternoon sun** catching the rim of his **sunglasses**.*

*"**Vignettes**," he says, waving at the **script** scattered across his **desk**. "Just **moments**, no **full story**—like **life**."*

*I **smirk**. "So... **lazy storytelling**?"*

"Sounds like lazy writing," Mayank replied with a smirk,

stirring his iced carrot juice.

A : Mayank, this is a warning ! Do not jump in between, especially when you are tweaking the details.

Mayank: ***Okay****, man! Whatever.*

Zubin grins. "Not lazy—economical for films. It's like life. You don't need everything to connect perfectly. Just show the moments. Let them breathe."

Mayank's spoon clinks against the glass. "Can it be poetic?"

"Why not?" Zubin shrugs. "Life's already poetry, if you look at it right."

I catch part of their conversation while typing out a clunky opening sentence for my abstract. I observe that there's a strange overlap between what I'm writing and what they're talking about—a structure that doesn't need to be complete, just meaningful.

"So, just... write what I see?" Mayank says aloud.

Zubin raises his sketchily acquired carrot juice in salute. "Exactly. No explanations, no expectations. Just vibes."

I return to my work, a small smile creeping onto my face. They might actually be onto something.

Mayank decides to try it—to capture the day in snapshots, letting the moments stand on their own, without forcing them to mean anything more.

The Highway Outside Manipal Residency

The ***road*** *dips lazily* ***downhill****, a slow stream of* ***asphalt***
flowing toward ***Udupi****, like it has nowhere important to*
be.
Cars *hum by, their* ***tires*** *hissing quietly over the* ***warm***
pavement*.*
A ***motorbike*** *zooms past, the* ***rider's scarf*** *flapping*
behind him,
like a ***ribbon*** *trying to make a break for it.*
The ***sun*** *scatters uneven patches across the* ***road****,*
shadows *stretching out—just long enough to disappear.*
Everything ***moves****, everything* ***shifts****.*
Moments *roll in and roll out,*
like ***waves on the shore****, here for a second—then, poof!*
Gone.
Ah, this moment!
Oops—gone.
That one?
Already slipped away, just like that.
It's like ***time****'s running a game I didn't sign up for,*
and I'm sitting here, watching all the ***good moments slip***
through,
like ***coins falling*** *through a* ***circular hole*** *in my pocket.*

Lunch with Zubin

Zubin *tears into the* ***Happy Meal box*** *like he's opening a* ***treasure chest****, his* ***sunglasses*** *pushed up on his* ***forehead****, sitting there like a makeshift* ***crown****. He's always had this* ***weird talent*** *for making* ***chaos look effortless****.*

"Can you believe it?" he mumbles, ***mouth full*** *of fries.*

"No more driving all the way to ***Mangalore*** *for a* ***Big Mac****."*

I let out a ***small, awkward laugh****—the kind that catches me off guard,*

like a ***sound*** *I haven't made in forever.* ***Rusty****, but still* ***mine****.*

It's funny how something as ***dumb*** *as a* ***fast-food delivery*** *could unlock a* ***laugh*** *I didn't know I had left.*

Zubin *holds up a* ***fry****, examining it like it's* ***artwork*** *on display.*

*"****Life's*** *all about the* ***small quests****, bro." He grins, tipping the* ***fry*** *towards me like a* ***toast****. "Even if the* ***reward*** *is just* ***fries****."*

The ***fries*** *are* ***soggy****, barely* ***warm****.*

The ***carrot juice*** *tastes like* ***regret****—liquid disappointment in a bottle.*

But ***weirdly****, it doesn't matter.*

There's something about sitting here, ***fries*** *in hand,* ***Zubin*** *being...* ***Zubin****, that makes it all feel* ***okay for the moment****.*

Rahul Arrives with Vastra (Clothes)

*The **door flies open**, and **Rahul** stumbles in, dragging a **sack** of clothes across the **floor**.*
***Dust** puffs up like it's been waiting all day for this **moment**, swirling **lazily** in the **sunlight**.*
***Rahul** smells like **temple air** and **incense sticks**—half **spiritual**, half **exhausted**.*
*"**Vastra** for the **gurdwara**," **Rahul** says, tossing the **sack** onto **Zubin's bed** like it's part of a **side mission**.*
*"**We'll drop them off tomorrow.**"*
***Zubin** lifts one **eyebrow**, the way only he can. "**Did you iron these?**"*
***Rahul** grins, brushing **dust** off his **sleeves** like he's walking off a **film shoot**.*
*"**Charity with dignity**, bro. **Always**."*
*The **sack** lands with a **thud**, sitting in the **corner**—*
*a **quiet promise**, waiting to be **fulfilled**.*
*It joins the other **things** in **life** that we **mean** to get to—**eventually**.*
***Rahul** claps his **hands** together. "**You in, Mayank?**"*
*I hesitate—just for a second, long enough to feel the **old version** of me hesitate too.*
*But this time, I **nod**. "**Yeah. I'll come.**"*

***Rahul** grins, brushing off more **dust** from his **sleeves**.*
*"**And what about the other Manipalite?**" He jerks his **chin** toward the **corner**, where **A**'s curled up in front of his **iMac**, headphones on, drowning in a **sea of papers**, **citations**, and **unfinished abstracts**.*
***Zubin** snickers. "**The dude's basically wallpaper at this point.**"*
*I glance over at **A**, watching him hover somewhere between **existing** and **disappearing**.*
*He doesn't move—just keeps **typing** away, like the **world outside** has **nothing** on whatever **paper** he's **working** on.*
*Same **room**. **Different orbits**.*

The People of Manipal

*The **late-night streets** of **Manipal** hum with **quiet**, **invisible life**, like a **song** missing half its **notes**—*
***unfinished** but still **playing**.*
*A **boy shuffles** along, dragging his **slippers** as if each **step** is heavier than the last.*
*He reminds me of **someone**—always carrying **something**, a **weight** that no one else can **see**, not even **him**.*
*A few steps away, a **girl** with oversized **headphones***
twirls,
*dancing to a **beat** only she can **hear**.*
*It's exactly the kind of **thing Anjali** would do—*

finding ***joy*** *in corners no one else* ***looks*** *in,* ***spinning*** *out of* ***sync*** *with the* ***world****, but not* ***caring****.*
The kind of ***person*** *who reminds you to* ***chase light****, even when there's* ***barely any****.*
At the ***closing chai stall****, a* ***couple*** *leans in too* ***close****,*
their ***voices low****,* ***sharp****, and full of* ***unfinished sentences****,*
like ***arguments*** *that need to* ***happen*** *but don't want to* ***end****.*
That's ***Rahul****—he doesn't* ***fight*** *for no* ***reason****.*
When he ***argues****, it's because he's trying to make* ***sense*** *of* ***something bigger****.*
Down the ***street****, on the* ***corner****, a* ***society-labeled*** *crazy vagabond plays a* ***flute****,*
his ***notes*** *drifting into the* ***air****—*
a ***melody*** *with no* ***destination****, meant to* ***wander****.*
It makes me think of ***Zubin****, the guy who always* ***follows life's tune*** *without worrying where it'll* ***take him****.*
He ***plays*** *his part without* ***expectations****, trusting that* ***everything*** *will* ***align eventually****.*
And me?
I guess I'm like the ***steam*** *from the* ***chai****—*
rising*,* ***swirling****,* ***fading****, and never* ***staying*** *anywhere long enough to* ***leave a mark****.*
Floating *through life, waiting for the* ***right moment*** *to arrive, but always* ***missing*** *it by just a* ***second****.*
The ***streets*** *of* ***Manipal*** *are full of* ***people*** *like us—*
all ***moving*** *in their* ***own rhythms****, toward or away from*

something.
*We're in the **same place**, but never quite **in sync**.*
*Like **moons** caught in **different orbits**, circling the **same planet** without ever **colliding**.*
*And maybe that's the **point**.*
*Maybe we don't have to **collide** to **matter**.*
*Maybe just **moving alongside** each other is **enough**.*

Hiding Today

***Rahul** hums a **tune**, tapping out an **off-beat rhythm** on the **table**—*
*slightly **out of sync**, but **steady** in its **own way**.*
***Zubin** scribbling **ideas** in the **margins** of his **screenplay**,*
*and the **researcher** glued to his **laptop**.*
*I pull the **black hoodie** with the **yellow Batman logo** tighter around me,*
*not because it's **cold**, but because it feels like **armor**—*
*something to **hold onto** when nothing else **fits**.*
*The **breeze** sneaks in through the **window**,*
*ruffling the **scattered papers** on **Zubin's desk**, as if the **day itself***
*wants to **rearrange** the **pieces** of my **life** without **asking first**.*
*It brushes past me, **light** and **indifferent**,*
*but I let it—it's easier to **float along** with it than **fight***

back.

I sit still, ***hoodie*** *drawn* ***tight,*** ***feet planted*** *on the* ***ground,***

but just ***barely.***

I'm not ***running yet,***

but at least I'm ***standing.***

Tomorrow?

Maybe I'll ***move.***

But ***today****?*

I'll just ***float.***

.

Across the room, *Mr.* ***Busy Bee's*** *fingers* ***pause*** *over the last* ***line*** *of his* ***abstract.*** *I* ***glance*** *over his* ***shoulder*** *and* ***read*** *it:* ***"Progress isn't defined by speed or scale—it's the quiet shift, the subtle promise that things will not stay as they are."***

The crescent moon dips lower into the night, casting faint silver streaks across the room. The air settles into a comfortable silence—the kind of silence that feels earned.

Rahul breaks it first, of course. "So, Gurdwara tomorrow?"

Zubin grins, already imagining tomorrow's conversations.

"Yeah. Research for Fiction."

The sack of vastra sits quietly in the corner—a promise

waiting for tomorrow, like everything else left unfinished.

And Mayank ?

He doesn't seem to be there yet. Not fully.

But that's okay.

Because the Waxing Crescent isn't about the light you already have—it's about the glimmer of what could be.

4. Waxing Crescent: Ripples in Time

To be paired with: ♪ **Time in a Bottle** - Jim Croce
Category: **Journal Entry**

Dear Journal,

I woke up late today, 8th of September ,as usual—**half the morning gone before I could catch it.** Zubin had texted in our WhatsApp group, a new plan for the morning:
"Quick shower at Arbi Falls ?"
Mayank agreed, almost too quickly—**like he didn't want to give himself time to back out.**
So, I went along, not because I wanted to hike, but because it felt easier than staying still.

Arbi Waterfalls (after a 4km Scooter Ride)

The trail to the falls is uneven—**part sun, part shadow**, weaving through trees like a thought that won't stay together. **Mayank walks ahead, quiet, hoodie pulled tight, hands shoved into his pockets.**

There are some things that cling to you—like **shadows stretching with the setting sun**. And **Mayank carries more than anyone should**, though I doubt he even realizes the weight. That's the scariest part—**he's gotten used to it.**

The blackmails. The late-night gynec visits. And those other moments—**abortions—silent thieves that steal pieces of your soul,** leaving you with nothing but **waiting rooms and half-spoken lies.**

The forest wraps us in stillness, broken only by the sound of water rushing downhill. We move through it slowly, the three of us noticing **the moss trailing along the creeks, water threading through fallen branches.**

Mayank is there, but not really. His silence speaks more than his words ever could.

At the base of the falls, the water crashes over rocks—**loud, relentless, indifferent.**

Mayank perches on a boulder, gazing at the spray like he's trying to see through it—**into a future he can't quite grasp.**

Zubin flips on his portable mic, recording the constant rhythm of water hitting stone.

"Ambience," he says, with a grin. "Even background noise matters."

So here is a bit of context: Back in our grad days, **Rahul developed this strange habit.** He would **hit up pubs and start philosophical debates**—recording everything on his

phone like he was hosting a personal talk show.
Conversations about **love, politics, ambition—whatever piqued his mood.**
At first, **Zubin thought it was all for show**, until he realized that **those messy, off-the-cuff conversations were gold**—the kind of moments you can't write; they just happen. **Now Zubin carries a mic everywhere**, catching bits of life like loose threads, waiting to be stitched into stories later.
The sun catches the spray just right—shards of glass floating in the air for a heartbeat before they're gone.
I think of **Jim Croce's song—if only we could save time in a bottle.**
But **you can't save moments,** can you? **All you can do is stand in them, hoping they'll mean something later.**

Gurdwara Sahib: Missing Keys and Misplaced Plans

By **midday**, we make it to the **Gurdwara Sahib.** Rahul and Anjali arrive first, waiting by the entrance. **But, of course, the sack of vastra we were supposed to bring is still sitting back in Zubin's room.**
And the **key to Zubin's room?**
Gone—lost somewhere on the trek.
The key had been tucked into **Mayank's fanny pack**, and **the fanny pack decided to go AWOL** sometime between the forest trail and our scooter ride back.
We spent an hour retracing our steps, turning over rocks, asking strangers—nothing.

Rahul wasn't thrilled. **"So, the vastra's locked inside? Fantastic."**
Zubin grinned, **"Look on the bright side: at least the key's enjoying the outdoors."**
Mayank just muttered, **"The universe really doesn't want me to have nice things."**
We had no choice but to **head to the gurdwara empty-handed.**

The air inside smelled like **incense and ghee**, and the stillness wrapped around us like a soft blanket. I don't know what it is about **the gurdwara**—but it makes everything **feel smaller, manageable.** Maybe that's the whole point—**to remind you that not everything has to be solved right away.**

Anjali sat cross-legged on the marble floor, scrolling through her phone, her nose ring catching the light. Rahul hovered near the door, tapping his foot. **"We'll just bring the vastras next week. Charity doesn't expire, right?"**
Zubin, never one to miss an opportunity, switched on his portable mic and slipped it into the pocket of his cargo lowers, capturing the subtle tension between us, like it was a piece of dialogue for his next screenplay.
Surprisingly, we all spread out—each of us gravitating toward a different corner of the hall, choosing solitude

over conversation.

The Sound of Devotion

A **bearded man sat at the center of the room, just behind the takht in the Darbar Sahib**, slowly waving a **white fly whisk—Chaur Sahib—over the Guru Granth Sahib.** His movements were fluid, almost hypnotic, as if he were stirring the air to cleanse it of everything unnecessary. The rhythmic motion reminded me of its use of '**Dhuno' (aromatic incense) at Durga Puja, the smoke weaving through the air, making the world feel sacred for a moment.**

Mayank sat quietly along the wall, his **white handkerchief loosely tied over his hair**, following the gurdwara tradition. His **fingers fidgeted with the sleeve of his hoodie**, twisting the fabric as if it held answers to questions he didn't know how to ask.

I nudged him gently.

"We'll figure it out. **It's just stuff.**"

He gave me a small nod—**the kind of nod that says, 'Not really, but maybe.'**

Two men sat on a raised platform, **their voices rising in shabad kirtan.** The boy on the **tabla** kept up a quick rhythm, while the vocalist, seated at the harmonium, sang with a depth that **made the air vibrate.** The **Granthi joined in, repeating the words,** creating a mesmerizing

back-and-forth:
Satnam, Satnam, Satnam...
Waheguru... Waheguru... Waheguru...
The notes swirled through the hall, **bouncing off the walls and sinking deep into the cool marble beneath our feet.** It wasn't just music—it was **a moment suspended in time,** a reminder that faith isn't always about answers but about the quiet courage to stay in the questions.
We bowed twice, following the rhythm of the service. **Some of the words resonated, some drifted past me ungrasped,**but it didn't matter. There was a stillness in the hall—a kind of weightless peace, as if the prayers knew **exactly where to land, soft and certain.** The entire congregation echoed in unison, **"Waheguru Ji Ka Khalsa, Waheguru Ji Ki Fateh"—said twice, echoed thrice.** It roughly translates to, *"Pure of the Lord are victorious,"* but the deeper meaning lies in its literal translation: **The Khalsa belongs to Waheguru, and so does the victory.**
From **shabad kirtan** (devotional hymns) to **paath** (reading from the Guru Granth Sahib), **ardas** (offered prayer), and **katha** (a story from the holy scripture), we stayed—heads bowed, hearts open, **immersed in the rhythm of devotion.**
When the service slowly phased out, **the air still hummed with a lingering reverence,** wrapping us in a peace that stretched beyond words. **We stood there a moment longer, absorbing it—letting the melodies and**

chants echo in our minds, long after the music had stopped.

That's when **Anjali leaned in, her nose brushing my shoulder,** and whispered:

"Let's now do what we're really here for—**free langar food.**"

Rahul, still halfway lost in thought, muttered aloud, **"Next time, we'll bring the clothes. No big deal."** His voice drifted in the stillness, light and unaffected.

Meanwhile, the locksmith was **caught up elsewhere—he'd be late for unlocking Zubin's Batcave.** So, we decided to **round off the day in the most wholesome way we could, with another random plan.**

And just like that, **the moment dissolved, replaced by a ripple of shared laughter—light and easy, like sunlight breaking through clouds.** This was us—**drifting through life, one misplaced key and one random plan at a time.**

On the Railway Bridge: Floating Forward

We ended the day on the old railway bridge, taking a short, muddy road off Parampalli Road, down the Coin Circle slope—**the far side of town, away from Manipal Residency.** The bridge stretched over the river, framed by **leaning coconut trees, their fronds sweeping the surface, trying to touch their own reflection.** We stood there, watching the soft, amber light of sunset slip into deeper hues. **The beams beneath us groaned underfoot** as if sharing their weary, silent endurance with us. **Shadows rippled on the water below**, dancing along with the fading light.

Anjali knew the bridge well—it had been a part of her early solo explorations, **before we all became friends.** But even she hadn't noticed the **rusty ladder bolted to the bridge's side**, hidden behind tangled vines. **The boys knew about it, of course.** It led to a **narrow steel platform, suspended beneath the tracks—just above the river, a secret world.** The kind of place you'd only find through exploration or mischief. The kind of place that **teen couples stumbled upon accidentally, hoping for a stolen moment.**

We climbed down one by one, the iron ladder protesting with every step—**old rust giving way but not quite enough to break.** There was a strange comfort in that creaking uncertainty, as if life itself was saying: **"Not smooth, but we're holding on."**

The platform wasn't much—just **a cold steel frame stretched beneath the bridge, hovering less than twenty feet above the river.** But down here, **it felt like a pocket of suspended time, a refuge tucked away from the world above.**The breeze was heavier, thick with salt and stories carried along the river's current. **Every sound we made bounced off the metal and echoed back, like a**

conversation with ourselves.

We sat cross-legged, our legs hanging over the edge, toes just a little too close to the flowing water. **The river murmured steadily beneath us**, and for the first time all day, Mayank seemed to breathe a little easier. **His hoodie, no longer pulled tight, slipped loosely around his shoulders.** His hands, which had clung to the fabric earlier like a lifeline, now rested open on his knees—**as if the weight he carried had shifted, if only for a moment.** In the background, **Rahul's phone was humming a remix cover " If words could make wishes come true, he would save every day like a treasure and then again," offbeat but unwavering.** That's what his aura was—**never quite in sync with the world but always present in it.** Zubin, naturally, had **his portable mic out, recording the sounds of the river and the bridge.**

Rahul grinned and called him out, "Sala, at-the-rate-memory-chor." Zubin just smiled and kept the mic running. That's how he saw life—**a collection of fragments waiting to be pieced together.** Moments others might forget, Zubin filed away, saved for scripts that might or might not ever be written.

And that's when **Rahul's phone buzzed.** He glanced at the screen, his face lit by the soft glow.

"The locksmith's at Zubin's place," he said, tucking his phone away. **"Guess your Batcave is safe after all."**

Zubin raised an eyebrow, that familiar grin sliding back into place. **"Well, look at that. We lost a key but found the night. Not bad."**

The **vastra—the charitiy clothes—would stay locked away for one more night**, but not every delay is a disaster.

Up on the bridge, the night folded into itself, the **crescent moon drawing a fine silver arc across the sky, like a whisper of something yet to come.** Below us, the river murmured softly, as if it carried secrets only it could understand. I sat alone for a moment, letting the day dissolve into the quiet hum of the water and the night breeze. **Time seemed to slow—just enough to hold this fleeting moment in its palm.**

And that's when we heard it—**a distant whistle, high and sharp, slicing through the night.**

The moving metal's pleasant noise could be hear coming closer to us.

Mayank sat up straight, a grin spreading across his face like a kid catching sight of fireworks.

"It's happening! Are you guys ready?"

Anjali's eyes widened. "What? What's happening?"

Zubin shot to his feet, fumbling to turn off his mic.

"Bhailog, let's move! Seriously, let's get up there!"

But **Mayank couldn't hold back his excitement.**

"**Wooohooo!**" he yelled, leaning forward over the edge, his voice echoing through the steel beams.

Anjali gasped, laughing and panicked all at once. "What

the hell—?!"

And then it hit.

KUUUUUUUUU.

The train horn blasted through the air, shattering the stillness like thunder. A wall of sound and motion roared over the bridge above us, **the steel beams groaning under its weight**. The world vibrated—**the bridge swayed, the cage beneath us shook**, and the river below shimmered with the impact. For a moment, we were suspended between the trembling iron and the swirling water—**caught between the earth and sky, between chaos and calm.**

Our voices disappeared into the roar of the train. The entire bridge became a living, breathing thing—**shaking, groaning, holding on just barely.**

Somewhere through the thunder, I caught fragments—**Mayank's exhilarated whoop, Rahul's nostalgic grin as he hummed along, Anjali's half-laugh, half-panic; and faint shout "Guchipudi".** In that moment, **we weren't thinking—we were just alive**, suspended in pure feeling, **the noise washing over us like a wave we didn't have to fight.**

And just as quickly as it came, the train was gone—**fading into the distance**, leaving behind a whisper of metal and motion.

The bridge stilled beneath our feet, the river below

rippling softly, as if breathing again.

We climbed back up the ladder in shifts, **the thrill still buzzing in our veins**, each of us holding onto the silence that followed.

Mayank pulled his hoodie off completely, draping it over his shoulder—**the tension he'd carried all day finally slipping away.** For the first time in what felt like forever, **he smiled—easy, unguarded.**

We stood on the bridge, quiet and content, **the moment settling into us like the cool night air.** The crescent moon hung above, soft and unassuming, like a promise—**not of answers, but of the space to float forward.**

September 8 | 8:55 PM

Yours Truly,

A

5. First Quarter: Stuck between here & there

To be paired with: ♪ **Vienna** - Billy Joel
Category: **Villanelle**

The first quarter moon *is like an* ***uncomfortable pause****—a place where everything feels* ***split****. Half of it* ***illuminated****, half in* ***shadow****, perfectly capturing what it feels like to* ***stand on the edge of something without stepping forward****.*

I've been in that ***in-between space*** *for too long—****stuck*** *between choices, waiting for a sign that never comes. It's not just about* ***Sindhu*** *or what came after. It's about how* ***life pulls you toward things and away from them****, leaving you suspended between moments.*

And that's what this phase feels like: ***standing in the middle of two stories****, unsure where one ends and the other begins.*

Stuck Between Here & There

The ***key's been found****, yet the* ***door won't unlock****,*
A ***moment of pause****, caught in* ***still air****.*

What's ***left behind****, what* ***waits on the clock****?*

Beneath that ***railway bridge****, we felt* ***time stop****,*
A ***train rattling over****, pulling thoughts* ***bare****.*
The ***key's been found****, yet the* ***door won't unlock****.*

Zubin's ***mic captured rivers*** *and* ***trains non-stop****,*
Stitching ***loose memories*** *we didn't declare.*
What's ***left behind****, what* ***waits on the clock****?*

Rahul joked about ***futures*** *and* ***timelines to mock****—*
Moving too ***slow*** *or* ***spinning elsewhere****.*
The ***key's been found****, yet the* ***door won't unlock****.*

Anjali sat ***still****, letting* ***ideas interlock****—*
Saying, "It's ***okay not to move everywhere****."*
What's ***left behind****, what* ***waits on the clock****?*

I stood ***silent****, heart full of* ***block****,*
A place ***stuck*** *between* ***desire*** *and* ***despair****.*
The ***key's been found****, yet the* ***door won't unlock****—*
What's ***left behind****, what* ***waits on the clock****?*

It's ***strange*** *how a* ***key*** *can be found, yet* ***everything still feels locked****. It's not really about* ***Zubin's Batcave****—or the* ***missing key****. It's about all the* ***things*** *that* ***refuse to move forward until you do****.*

The **climb under the railway bridge** *felt like that—a* **suspended space***, a moment* **stolen** *from everything else, like* **life gave us permission to pause***. The* **river moved beneath us***, the* **train passed above***, and for a few minutes, the* **world let us exist between its layers***.*

We ended the night **back at Zubin's place***. The* **locksmith** *finally showed up, his* **tired hands working the lock** *until it gave way with a* **quiet click***. Zubin* **swung the door open with a grin***, as if* **unlocking the room** *meant unlocking something* **bigger***.*

"See?" Rahul said, clapping me on the back. "Not everything stays **stuck forever***."*

Zubin threw his hands up **dramatically***, "Another* **crisis, solved***. Time for some MacD and* **fries***?"*

The **sack of vastra** *was still waiting—***delayed** *but not forgotten. And in that moment, it felt like* **everything** *we'd been carrying—***keys, clothes, or memories***—didn't need to be* **resolved** *right away.*

Maybe the **moon knows** *something we don't—that* **every phase** *is just a* **preparation for the next***. And maybe being* **stuck isn't failure***—it's just a* **quiet reminder to**

breathe *before the* ***next step****, and ask yourself, "****Are you happy?****"*

6. Half Moon : The Mirage of HappYness

To be paired with: ♪ **Welcome Chris** - Andrea Guerra
(Movie: The Pursuit of Happyness)
Category: **An Academic Abstract**

The Mirage of Happiness: Academic Disillusionment, Love Lost, and the Fragile Pursuit of Meaning

Keywords: happiness, academic disillusionment, personal heartbreak, liminality, pursuit of happiness, fleeting moments, resilience

Introduction

Happiness, as a concept, is often sold as a promise of fulfilment, achieved through success, love, or stability. Yet, in academia and matters of the heart, this promise is frequently broken. This paper examines the elusive nature of happiness, drawing parallels between the struggles faced by PhD scholars navigating a challenging system and lovers dealing with the remnants of failed relationships. Using *The Pursuit of Happyness* (Muccino, 2006) as a narrative lens, this exploration seeks to capture the resilience required to persist when happiness appears beyond reach. The protagonist, Chris Gardner, exemplifies the relentless pursuit of a better life amidst profound challenges—a pursuit mirrored by scholars seeking acknowledgement and lovers seeking closure.

The Scholar's Pursuit: Navigating Academic Disillusionment

For PhD scholars dependent on stipends, the act of pausing studies through a Loss of Payment (LOP) leave often carries devastating consequences. What begins as a necessary break to address personal crises can devolve into an extended period of exile, marked by financial insecurity, bureaucratic delays, and diminished guidance from supervisors. The promise of returning to the familiar rhythms of academic life is quickly replaced by a harsh reality where progress is measured against rigid institutional timelines, leaving many scholars feeling adrift. In this academic purgatory, happiness becomes fragile and perpetually deferred. Bauman's (1997) concept of a liquid modern world, where stability is illusory, resonates with the struggles of scholars whose hopes are continuously postponed.

This disillusionment parallels the experience of failed lovers. Just as scholars seek validation and guidance, lovers seek closure and understanding. Both are often left navigating a sea of unmet expectations, learning to survive on echoes of what could have been. Happiness becomes a moving target—"I'll feel better when I get my stipend back" or "I'll be fine once I stop missing them." In reality, as *The Pursuit of Happyness* illustrates, the path to fulfilment is fraught with moments of despair and uncertainty, punctuated by small, often unnoticed victories.

Happiness as a Mirage: Between Grief and Survival

In both academia and love, happiness often appears as a mirage—seemingly within reach but dissolving upon closer inspection. The scholar burdened by financial instability and a lack of meaningful guidance finds their joy slowly slipping away, each research milestone marred by setbacks. Similarly, the failed lover replays memories of conversations and missed opportunities, hoping for closure that may never come. As Haidt (2006) argues, true happiness is not the absence of struggle but the ability to navigate through it. Both the scholar and the lover must learn to live with their grief, folding it into their daily lives.

This is where fleeting moments of grace come into play.

Happiness, as Ahmed (2010) suggests, is often found not in grand achievements but in small, unnoticed moments. For the scholar, it may be the satisfaction of a single paragraph that finally makes sense. For the heartbroken lover, it might be a fleeting laugh, a sunset, or a familiar song that briefly lightens the burden. Much like Chris Gardner's brief moments of respite in *The Pursuit of Happyness*, these instances of grace remind us that happiness is not a fixed destination but a shifting state, experienced in moments that break through the darkness.

Finding Grace in Fleeting Moments

Happiness, as articulated in Osho Jain's *Khush Toh Hai Na* (2020), is a question suspended in ambiguity—"Are you happy?" The answer remains elusive, capturing the liminal space occupied by both scholars and lovers. Zubin's habit of recording conversations, capturing moments others would let slip away, embodies this idea. These recordings, like Jain's song, preserve fleeting joys and echoes of what once was. The scholar and the lover must learn to collect such moments, using them as breadcrumbs to navigate their uncertain paths.

The Pursuit of Happyness(2006) underscores the importance of finding meaning in moments of struggle. Chris Gardner's journey is a testament to resilience—not through grand gestures but through small acts of persistence. Scholars and lovers must similarly find strength in brief flashes of clarity—a completed page, a shared smile—reminders that their struggles are not in vain.

Conclusion: Floating Through Life's In-Betweens

Both the scholar without a stipend and the lover without closure exist in a liminal state—between hope and disillusionment, longing and acceptance. Nhat Hanh (1999) reminds us that happiness is not a destination but a way of being present with what is. For the scholar, this may mean accepting that not every project will reach its envisioned conclusion. For the heartbroken lover, it may mean learning to carry their grief lightly, like a scar that no longer aches but never fully fades.

Progress, as the narrative of *The Pursuit of Happyness* suggests, is not defined by speed or scale—it is the quiet shift, the subtle promise that things will not stay as they are. By trusting in this shift, both scholars and lovers can find hope amidst uncertainty, moving forward not because they have found happiness but because they are learning to live with its absence.

In the end, the scholar and the lover share a common pursuit—chasing happiness as if it were something to be found, only to realise that it has always existed within them, hidden in quiet moments of resilience and fleeting grace. As Jain's song asks, "Khush toh hai na (**Are you happy**)?"—the question remains open, inviting reflection on the spaces between joy and sorrow, between what is and what could be.

References

Ahmed, S. (2010). *The promise of happiness.* Duke University Press.

Bauman, Z. (1997). *Postmodernity and its discontents.* Polity Press.

Dostoevsky, F. (1994). *Notes from underground* (R. Pevear & L. Volokhonsky, Trans.). Vintage Books. (Original work published 1864)

Frankl, V. E. (2006). *Man's search for meaning.* Beacon Press. (Original work published 1946)

Haidt, J. (2006). *The happiness hypothesis: Finding modern truth in ancient wisdom.* Basic Books.

Jain, O. (2020). Khush toh hai na [Song]. Independent release. Available on Spotify and Apple Music.

Muccino, G. (Director). (2006). *The pursuit of happyness* [Film]. Columbia Pictures.

Nhat Hanh, T. (1999). *The heart of the Buddha's teaching: Transforming suffering into peace, joy, and liberation.* Harmony Books.

Seligman, M. E. P. (2011). *Flourish: A visionary new*

understanding of happiness and well-being. Free Press.

Submission Date: September 11th

7. Waxing Gibbous: Light and Lines

To be paired with: ♪ **Daylight** - David Kushner
Category: **Sestina**

***Mr. A** had made us come to an **early evening tea**. **Rahul** and **Anjali** ditched us for their **Mallu love of coffee**, which was also available at **Chai Point**, but it is not easy to explain how their brains 'brain' (a reference game). **Chai Point** had the kind of atmosphere that easily blends into the **background**, just like us. It sat across the road from **Jewel Rock**—a small, quiet bar, tucked into shadows, with its **half-lit sign** blinking softly above a dark entrance. **Jewel Rock** wasn't the kind of place people went to be seen; it was where they slipped in quietly, unobserved, letting the dim light and **smoky corners** hold whatever weight they brought in. We'd ended up opposite to it, drawn to the **calm** of the spot, the promise of **chai**, and the way we could speak low, uninterrupted.*

***Mr. A** leaned back, tapping his **pen** against his **notebook**. He'd been helping me find ways to **ground myself in writing**, sensing the tension I'd been carrying—a weight of things **left unsaid**. Between **sips of tea**, he traced a*

word onto his napkin *and looked over at me. "Ever tried a* ***Sestina****?" he asked, eyes fixed, awaiting a response.* ***Six stanzas****,* ***six lines each****, and a final* ***three-line envoi****, he explained, witnessing my blank look for a* ***micro-minute****. "It's not about getting to the point right away," he added. "It's about letting certain things come back, settling into different places until they feel right."*

Zubin *had made himself comfortable with taking* ***non-consensual voice recordings*** *of others. I chose to ignore him and refocused my thoughts on what* ***Mr. A*** *was saying.*

The thought of letting ***words revisit themselves*** *felt like* ***permission*** *to approach things I'd been holding at arm's length. The* ***repetition****, the* ***slow build****—maybe it was exactly the kind of structure I'd needed. Like walking through* ***familiar thoughts****, only to see them from new* ***angles****—softer, easier to face.*

So, with ***Mr. A's napkin scribble*** *guiding me, I picked up the* ***pen****. I leaned into the* ***words****, letting them* ***circle*** *and* ***settle****, hoping that in time, I might feel just as at* ***ease****.*

Light & Lines

In a ***quiet cafe****,* ***pen scratches paper****,* ***words held tight****,*

*The **evening air** thick with questions, as **shadows fold**,*
*I watch **ink blurs** and settles, **memory's pull strong**,*
*Lines unfurl, pulling me back and forward, a **circle unending**,*
*Where each moment shifts between **healing** and **grief's reign**,*
*My **hand steady** now, words like **walls** I learn to **trust**.*

*A once **fragile spirit** finds lines, places of comfort to **trust**,*
*Through the **page**, I hear a faint, steady hum, a **safe light***
*For the dusk I feared might forever bear **sorrow's reign**.*
*Now, in **small verses**, in spaces where **meaning folds***
*And unfolds, I chart a path, moving toward an **ending**,*
*Breaking gently from **memory's unrelenting pull**.*

*The **page** is a mirror, each line another tether's **pull**,*
*Tying my scattered thoughts, a guide my heart can **trust**.*
*In the rhythm of **words**, I lose the dark's **unkind ending**,*
*Hold close the promise of **dawn**, a fragile, familiar **light***
*That softens the **silence**. I let go, my fears **fold***
*Away, as I sketch new constellations, **dreams reign**.*

*Where **memory** once held me, it no longer **reigns**,*
*Each **page** turned, each word written eases the **pull**,*
*And slowly, softly, my **silence** into **whispers folds**—*
*Words exchanged and kept, steady **pillars of trust**.*

*I write through the **dark**, ink casting a hopeful **light**,*
*Tracing my way through **shadow** to find an **ending**.*

*The **future**, undefined but felt, an unspoken **ending**,*
*Is held in my hand like the soft, unassuming **reign***
*Of dawn breaking, casting its **resilient light***
*Over **ink-stained hands**, loosing the past's **pull**.*
*Between lines, I build a steadying **trust**,*
*Shapes of **peace**, a shelter in words I **fold**.*

*In **silence** we sit, two friends where **memory folds***
*Around us, untangling threads, a quiet **ending**,*
*One guiding, one guided, bound in the same **trust**.*
*Outside, stars hold the sky, a gentle **reign***
*Of constellations marking my **pulse's pull**,*
*Each one a reminder, a small, soft **light**.*

*So I write, **pages** and **pauses holding light**, lines **fold***
*Into **stories** that hold me **safe**, past's **pull** finds an **ending**.*
*A steady **reign** of words and **trust**, as healing takes hold.*

*"Some things, you **bend**, until they **fit**, or you find a new way to **try**.", somewhere in between, while I was writing, **Mr. A** said. As I reflect, I understand we both carry our **losses**; his break another **hold**. I get it too well—when the heart **pulls low**, even familiar things feel hard to rest.*

The weight of ***regret pulls*** *me from any* ***rest****, memories* ***bending*** *each thought towards an* ***end****. I didn't choose a place left* ***heavy and low****. For* ***A****, it's a different* ***loss****—a dream deferred but still worth the* ***try****. He's here, waiting for life to tell him when to move, hoping this time will offer a steadier* ***hold****.*

So we sit, both working to keep some ***hold****, on what seems too fragile to let* ***rest****, following the* ***sestina's beat*** *to see what might move. A pattern circles back, teaching words to* ***bend****, to hold their place without forcing an answer to* ***try****—just seeing how* ***loss*** *might* ***heal****, even if slow.*

Outside, ***daylight fades****, slipping* ***low****. We* ***bend****, letting* ***loss*** *find* ***rest****, giving* ***trust*** *another* ***try****.*

8. Waxing G: Shadows Beneath the Glow

To be paired with: ♪ **Saturn** - Sleeping at Last
Category: Dostoyevskian Rant

Hey there! Now that we have your attention, no more words in bold, until Mr. A feels like. We would appreciate your full focus. Read between the lines; take in every word. And I hope you're following the audio instructions as you go along.

The streets buzz with a kind of mindless movement, a parody of progress. Everyone around me walks as if they're on a tightrope only they can see, every step heavy with self-importance. Their faces are masks of hurried determination, their glances darting past each other as if afraid to make contact, to acknowledge their own fragility reflected back. They pretend that they matter more, that their strides leave deeper imprints, as if the weight of their presence could reshape the very ground beneath them. It's all so convincing, this lie we live, and I can't help but wonder about the origin of this delusion. Dostoevsky asked, "Oh, do tell me who first announced, who first proclaimed that man only does vile things because he doesn't know his own true interests;

that if he were enlightened and his eyes were opened to his real, normal interests, man would at once become virtuous and noble?" I can't escape this thought. The promise of enlightenment has shackled us more than ignorance ever could, trapping us in a cycle of self-importance masked as self-awareness.

I have spent countless hours chasing meaning, consuming theories, and immersing myself in ideas that promised answers, hoping they would offer a path out of the murk of confusion. But the more I learn, the heavier the weight becomes, as if every piece of knowledge drives me deeper into some suffocating abyss. It's as if each revelation, instead of illuminating, only casts more shadows, leading me down paths that twist and turn but never open into clarity. Understanding is no ladder—it's a spiral staircase, and with every step, the way back seems further lost. They say that knowledge is power, but no one speaks of its curse—how it strips you of blissful certainty and replaces it with questions that never rest, how it burrows deep and roots itself in your bones, making it impossible to forget the burden of knowing too much.

The pursuit of meaning feels like a cruel trick, a hall of mirrors where every reflection distorts what you thought you knew. We reach out desperate to grasp some semblance of truth, but each piece we seize turns brittle and breaks apart in our hands. There is no escape from this quest, no way to unlearn the burden of wanting to know. The haunting lyrics of Hotel California echo in my mind: "You can check out any time you like, but you can never leave." Enlightenment is no different—a seductive promise that, once entered, leaves no path back. We enter willingly, convinced that answers will liberate us, only to find ourselves bound tighter by the very chains we sought to break.

There are moments, rare and fleeting, when clarity feels almost within reach—like a whisper of a truth too grand to hold. I think of those words: "I couldn't help but ask for you to say it all again." There are truths, rare as comets in a dark sky, that you grasp for but can never quite hold. The words slip like sand through my fingers, and I am left grasping at the emptiness where meaning should be. I tried to capture it once—tried to write it down, to immortalize the feeling that the universe was made just to be seen by my eyes. But the pen failed me, and every attempt to crystallize the moment left it more fractured than before. It is the human curse: to know that the most profound revelations are also the most fleeting, slipping beyond reach the moment you seek to possess them.

Mayank is no stranger to this struggle. I see him every day, caught between ambition and failure, burdened by the weight of every "what if" and every missed opportunity. He moves through life like a man navigating a stormy sea, hoping that the next wave will carry him to shore but knowing, deep down, that the current is too strong. He's like me in ways I never wanted to admit—hoping that knowledge or purpose would offer a path out of the dark, only to find it more labyrinthine than ever. Both of us, drifting under the waxing gibbous moon, grasping at fragments of light that never seem to make us whole. We chase meaning as if it's a star to be captured, but every step brings new questions, new fractures.

The moon tonight hangs heavy in the sky—more than half full but not quite complete. Its light is deceptive, casting long shadows that dance and shift, never revealing the whole truth. It serves as a reminder that we, too, are always almost there but never quite arriving. Progress is promised, but its pace is slow, its glow uneven. We chase enlightenment, love, meaning—whatever we think will fill the void—but all we do is layer shadows atop shadows. We trick ourselves into believing that we are advancing, but in reality, we are running in circles, trapped by our own need to make sense of the chaos.

The stars above remind me of what I cannot hold, of what I've lost. "The universe was made just to be seen by my eyes"—a moment of cosmic grandeur, a fleeting sense of purpose in a vast, uncaring expanse. But even this thought slips through my grasp like water through clenched fists. To have witnessed even a glimmer of that beauty is both a gift and a torment—an awareness that makes every subsequent step feel heavier, every breath more burdened by what is just out of reach.

Perhaps that's why I write this—not because I have answers or hope to find them, but because it's the only way to sift through the noise, to rage against the illusion, to peel back the layers and stare into the abyss, even if it stares back. To question why we believed that knowledge, love, or meaning would heal us when all it has done is make the fractures more visible. Mayank sits across from me, silent, his thoughts hidden behind half-smiles and tired eyes. We share this burden—bound by the same questions, circling the same gibbous light, hoping one day it might just make sense. The silence between us speaks louder than words, a quiet acknowledgement of our shared despair and the faint hope that somewhere, somehow, there is more than this. Until then, we write, we think, we rage—and we float beneath the moon's half-hearted promise of illumination, caught between the shadows and the light, forever seeking and never finding, but unable to stop the search. We press on, because what else is there to do? It is both our curse and our salvation—to be creatures who hope against hope, who fight even when the fight seems futile. And like the stars that whisper secrets we may never fully understand, we hold our light, however fragile, against the darkness, knowing that even if the universe was made to be seen by our eyes, we are only scratching the surface of its infinite depth. We are both guests and prisoners, entering willingly but perhaps never truly leaving.

I have tried to capture it all before—to make sense of the chaos and give it meaning. I have tried to write it down, to hold the fleeting truths in my hands, but **I could never find a pen.**

Pen found on: September 16th

9. Waning Crescent Cradles

♪ **Super Collide** - Banners
Category: Elegy

I.

The sky dims softly; shadows bend and sway,
A quiet grief now anchors in my chest.
Our love's remains—what we chose to betray,
Lie fractured, brittle, never laid to rest.
We parted ways on terms that felt like peace,
Yet lies you told sank deep and split our bond.
I swallowed every untruth for release;
Though bitterness within me lingered long.

II.

I still recall the silent words we shared,
The way you pulled the truth beneath a veil.
Twice you held ***secrets we had never dared—***
A bond reshaped by lies that would prevail.

You claimed another path, another cause;
You severed ties before I knew to grieve.
Yet I was bound, entwined by unseen laws—
Hate's grip so strong, Love had to leave.

III.

Do you remember when we burned so bright,
When every touch felt endless and complete?
Now I recoil from memories of night—
The ashes of our past lie at my feet.
Hate was not born of love, but what it broke—
A slow decay that twisted hope to pain.
I carried words too heavy to be spoke,
Each syllable of sorrow etched with strain.

IV.

The waning crescent cradles bitter truth—
A waning light for shadows left to grow.
To hold your lies and all that you outgrew
Is to hold fire that burns both high and low.
***Supercollide**—our hearts in reckless flame,*
Yet aftermath leaves nothing but regret.
Each whispered threat, each call in hidden shame,
Blackmail's dark tether binds me to its net.

V.

*Yet **moons will wane and rise,** though scars remain,*
Their light a path that leads beyond this grief.
To hold the darkness close is to sustain
A wound that finds no end, no sweet relief.
I mourn the life, the love, the lost and gone—
A hope turned brittle in a bed of thorns.
I lay this weight to rest before the dawn,

And let the crescent cradle my reborn.

A Note for You: Dear Co-Orbiters

While you process the elegy, the curiosity in the human mind may make us jump and pinpoint what appears to be a falter in the flow—"No, it is the full moon that comes after the waxing gibbous." Yes, we know. The expected sequence is clear, like the count of numbers—1, 2, 3, 4—each phase moving with predictable precision. But life, emotions, and healing rarely follow such simple order; they often move in a rhythm that defies linearity. Sometimes, it's 1, 2, 3, 4, and then suddenly, 8, 7, 6, 5. The path is tangled, and the light we seek does not always come in the way we anticipate.

Moving on, confronting loss, and finding meaning in pain is never a straightforward journey. It is as if the moon, instead of shining its expected fullness after hope has swelled, recedes into shadows. The waxing gibbous suggests a nearing of completion—a culmination of all the light gathered. But instead, there is the waning crescent—a place where shadows linger longer and the light wanes just as it felt within grasp. Here, wounds are raw, truths are bitter, and hope flickers in uncertainty.

Healing is not linear; it is a winding path, full of stops and starts, of regression and renewal. We cannot force the phases to align perfectly with our desires, but we can honour the cycle that brings us from darkness to light again and again.

This completeness does not erase the journey—the waxing and waning, the rise and fall—but it acknowledges that through the cycles, through each stumble and return, there is the possibility of light and wholeness again.

10. Waning Crescent: Quiet Reflections

♪ **Night Changes** - One Direction
Category: **Haiku at the End**

The air was heavy with a stillness that only comes when night begins to surrender to the early whispers of dawn. We had gathered on the balcony of Angel's Court, an old Manipal apartment complex that seemed to exist in its own slow-moving time, overlooking the patchwork of lights that stretched toward Udupi town. The sky was a vast canvas of deep indigo, the waning crescent moon clinging to its faint light—a fragile, curved promise.

The celebration of the night, in honor of Anjali's Scopus publication, had left Mayank in a deep, unbothered sleep inside his room. The four of us, though—Rahul, Anjali, Zubin, and me—found ourselves on the balcony, each carrying our own silences. Anjali curled up on a rusted metal chair, her eyes tracing constellations she could name but never quite touch. Rahul flicked the last embers of his cigarette into the void, the faint glow snuffed out before it met the ground. "You ever feel like you're stuck on the edge of something?" he asked, his voice low and introspective, as if sharing a secret with the night itself.

Zubin, typically quick with comebacks, was quiet tonight. He leaned against the cool railing, headphones draped loosely around his neck, ready to capture everything and nothing. It felt as though we were standing at the brink of some unseen change. The waning crescent moon above seemed to reflect our state —a sliver of light slipping into darkness, not out of defeat but as a prelude to something new.

"Rahul's right," Anjali said softly, a smile playing on her lips. "Sometimes it feels like everything's just... waiting." We nodded, each of us weighing our unspoken thoughts. I sipped my chai, the warmth grounding me as I considered the question. So many moments lately had felt like pauses stretched into permanence. For me, the last few months had been nothing but that—silent spaces in which I held my breath, not sure whether to move forward or hold back.

Zubin adjusted the mic in his pocket, capturing the late-night ambiance—the faint **chirp** of crickets, the soft **rustle** of leaves, and the gentle sound of chai being **sipped**, punctuating the silence.
"You know," Anjali began, her voice light but tinged with something thoughtful, "Rachel's coming to stay with

me."
"Rachel?" Zubin raised an eyebrow, feigning ignorance. "Is that your long-lost cousin or..."
"Her husky," I said, a grin tugging at my lips. "Anjali's pride and joy."

"Oh, right. The blue-eyed beaut," Rahul spoke, leaning back and giving a sarcastically remarked "Kerala's finest export."
Anjali rolled her eyes, but her smile grew. "My fiancé's parents are travelling, and 'J' is in South Africa for work. So... I'm on this Siberian's duty."

"Ah," Zubin said, eyes lighting up with mock seriousness. "A test of worthiness! They're measuring your caretaking skills. Handle Rachel well, and maybe—just maybe—they'll let you take care of their precious 'J.'"

Rahul grinned, nearly spilling his chai. "Imagine failing the dog test. 'Sorry, you're great, but Rachel didn't approve. No wedding bells for you.'"
Anjali laughed, a sound that rang out clear and genuine. "If Rachel's more of a diva than me, I'm doomed."
"You? A diva?" I exclaimed.
Rahul nodded in mock agreement. "You're the least diva person here, bro."
"Anjali's the bro-est of bros, like Monica" Zubin added,

breaking his silence, to triangulate the data.
Rahul and I, gave Zubin a concerned look. Zubin defended himself by saying, "I mean... the OCD!"

“I do not know, whether to be happy about it or sad” Anjali said with laugh held at the back of her throat. We all joined Anjali in the 10 second due laugh.

“We’re all growing up too fast. Feels like yesterday I met A in front of the MIC (College) water cooler.” Rahul said, his tone suddenly serious. I glanced at him, acknowledging his sentiment with a small smile. The laughter faded, but the warmth lingered.
Zubin cleared his throat, his voice steady but distant. “Change is funny. It never shows up the way you think.”

He was right. Life had a way of circling back to what we thought we’d left behind. Like Mayank, always wrestling with memories, searching for a way forward. And me? My academic break, intended as a pause to find clarity, had only complicated things. Stepping away meant facing parts of myself I had d tried to bury. Coming back meant reconciling who I was with who I wanted to be.

“Do you ever think,” Rahul said, his gaze on the same stars now, “that letting go isn’t hard because of what you lose, but because of what it leaves behind?”

His words lingered in the air. Letting go isn't just about release; it's about facing the void left behind. It's learning to exist in those quiet spaces.
I thought of Mayank—of his heartbreak, of the weight he carried. I thought of myself, navigating paths both chosen and forsaken. Maybe we were all learning to let go, each in our own way.
The moon dipped lower, a sliver of light barely hanging on. Fragile yet resilient. A reminder that darkness isn't an end, just a transition.

Rahul broke the silence with a laugh. "Enough heavy stuff. What's next? We can't stare at the moon forever."
Zubin slipped his headphones on. "Speak for yourself."
Anjali's eyes stayed on the stars. "I wish I had money for a flight to see J."
I caught her sentiment and added, "I wish I had funds for my PhD fieldwork."
Rahul smirked. "I wish I could find a producer for my film."
Zubin raised a finger with mock gravity, an exaggerated look of solemnity crossing his face. "I wish... I didn't finish the last Shawarma. Now who will save my soul?"

Rahul nearly choked on his chai. "Truly tragic. A shawarma-less life. You'll be remembered in our thoughts and prayers."

Anjali groaned, shaking her head with a smile. “And here I was, thinking you had deep, meaningful wishes.”

Zubin placed a hand over his heart, eyes wide. “Hey, Shawarmas are the epitome of depth. Layers of sauces, hidden spices... They reflect life’s Guchipudis.”

“Stop before I cry,” I said, unable to hold back my laughter. “Shawarma philosophy, folks. Only here, only now.”

Rahul leaned back, grinning. “And that’s why we’re doomed. Shawarma philosophers, chai addicts, and dog-test survivors. The future is bright.”

Zubin lifted his empty chai cup as if making a toast. “To tragic Shawarmas and unpredictable futures!”

We clinked our cups together—empty, half-full, and barely touched—letting the laughter and late-night air hold whatever came next.

As I clinked, I weaved in my mind, a few words, like a —

Haiku

In night’s quiet sigh,
Dreams weave through shadows and light—
Change whispers, “Not yet.”

Saved in Notes: September 27th

11A. Third (quarter) Moon's Toast

♪ **Moondust***(Stripped; EP version) - Jaymes Young*
Category: **Roundel**

Another night had pulled us together again, like it always seemed to—no planned occasion, no formal gathering. Just one of those moments where the world outside felt too heavy, and we instinctively gravitated towards each other. Tonight, it was Zubin's idea, as he claimed to have "the perfect playlist for existential crises," a phrase that only made Rahul roll his eyes and Anjali laugh. Zubin, ever the observer and chronicler, was focused today on output, setting up his speaker in a wall corner to create the perfect reverb. Anjali, engrossed in a book of quotes, occasionally flicked glances our way—glances that seemed to pierce through the surface but never judged. And then there was Mr. A—steady, unassuming, the glue that held us together whenever life tried to pull us apart.

A surge of gratitude welled up inside me—a warmth that cut through the chill of the late-night air. It wasn't the ***double malt on rocks*** *or the three-quarters-down glasses that kept me anchored this time; it was them. This* *makeshift family, this ragtag group, who made all of it bearable. I had walked through darkness—stumbled along the paths of heartbreak and regret—but here, in their presence, I could breathe again. I could almost taste freedom from sorrow, slipping gently into something that resembled hope.*

Raising my glass—once meant for whiskey but now filled with fruit-infused water in honour of healthier choices—I let the moment linger. A toast not to the drink but to them. To the friends who refused to let me drown.

I started to read aloud the roundel I'd written the night before, the words echoing softly in the quiet:

Third Moon's Toast

The third moon fades; glass touched by light,
Double malt on rocks, three quarters deep—
Bottoms up to bury loss in sleep,
To drown the ache of endless night.
With every sip, the shadows bite,
Yet solace lies not where spirits seep.
The third moon fades; glass touched by light,
Double malt on rocks, three quarters deep.

But now the moon's waning invite

Speaks of release, no tears to keep—
With FRIENDS who hold me as I leap,
The Ross-and-Joey, guide through plight.
Anjali's care, a Monica's might;
Rahul's Phoebe flair, Zubin's quip steep.
The third moon fades; glass touched by light,
This phase now mine, my heart's own sweep.

As Mayank finished, Zubin's portable speaker came to life, filling the air with an unexpected tenderness. The opening notes of "Moondust" drifted out, catching us all off guard—a rare, unspoken softness from him. The melody wrapped around us like a shared secret, as if the night had finally decided to let its guard down.

"I'm building this house on the moondust," the lyrics whispered, each word catching on the wind and settling somewhere deep within. For a moment, it felt like the scattered fragments of our lives—the broken memories, the regrets we tried to bury—found their place. Not in perfect symmetry, but in a way that made sense, if only for now. I glanced at the faint shimmer of the waning moon, fragile and low—a reminder that even as its light dimmed, renewal was possible.

I turned my eyes back to my friends; my FRIENDS, as per the analogy drawn by Mayank. Rahul, mid-joke, with words half-spoken but contagious in their humor. Anjali's laughter, unrestrained and genuine. Zubin, uncharacteristically quiet, immersed in his own rhythm. And our very own Ross- Mr. Mayank Agarwal, the hopeless romantic, leaning against the wall, after delivering a decent roundel.

"I'm hiding from the truth, that it's all in my mind," the song continued, brushing over wounds I had grown used to hiding. But tonight, it felt different—less a weight to carry, more a map to follow. Moondust wasn't a grave for what was lost; it was the ground on which I could rebuild, piece by hesitant piece.

"Guess we're all moondust in some way," I murmured, mostly to myself, but loud enough for the night to catch and carry.

Mr. A, ever perceptive, raised his tea cup in a silent toast, his smile soft and knowing. "Aren't we all?" he said, tapping his cup against an imaginary glass in my hand—a small gesture that spoke volumes. It was a toast to scars, to imperfections, and to moving forward one step at a time.

As the music continued to weave its spell around us, I let it wash over me like a gentle tide, smoothing the jagged edges of the past. I thought about the path I'd travelled—the missteps, the sleepless nights, and the small victories that somehow kept coming.

As the last notes of "Moondust" faded softly into the night, Rahul leaned in......

11B. The Other Half

♪ **Back To The Sky** (Ft. JFDR) or **So Far**- Ólafur Arnalds
Category: **Pallindromes**

As the last notes of "Moondust" faded softly into the night, Rahul leaned in with a spark in his eyes—the kind that promised another of his whimsical cosmic facts. “Did you know,” he began, voice hovering between playful and serious, “Earth is about to gain a second moon—2024 PT5?”

Anjali tilted her head, a mix of curiosity and disbelief flashing across her face. It was an expression best captured as “Aaan?”—a sound hanging somewhere between intrigue and scepticism.

I jumped in, unable to resist adding to the moment. “It’s an asteroid, temporarily caught by Earth’s gravity. Just hanging around for a while, making its rounds, then slipping away again.”

Zubin’s chuckle was a dry, knowing laugh. “So, even the universe dabbles in casual flings,” he quipped. “A temporary dance with a rock before letting it drift.”

Our laughter bubbled up—unrestrained, again. genuine, carving out a brief moment of lightness that pushed away the weight of the night. But as the echoes faded, a lingering thought took root. There's something both poetic and bittersweet about a temporary moon—a reminder of how even passing connections leave their mark, changing us in ways we barely understand.

As Zubin's speaker shifted to a gentle, lyrical instrumental, the conversation faded, leaving a soft stillness in the air. I leaned back, letting the echoes of laughter dissipate into the night. My new supervisor's words lingered in my mind: "I see potential in your work," they'd said. "But you have to commit fully. No half-measures." Encouragement, rare as it was, came with a price—more hours, greater sacrifice, and the absence of financial security. The familiar weight of academic pursuit pressed heavily, a reminder of what it demanded. I couldn't help but see a reflection of my struggle in Mayank's journey—both of us piecing together fragments of ourselves, uncertain of what it would ultimately cost.

As Mayank sought to rebuild himself, I too faced the daunting prospect of starting anew. Could I afford the risks? Could I bear the financial strain, the relentless demands of academia, and the stakes of giving my all, including my hard-earned GPA of 9.6?

I exhaled deeply, opened a notepad on my e-device, and

began to write.

Cyclic P.

Time slips by—
Moon wanes, shadows sigh.
Alone, light fades; hope's fleeting cry.
Cycles of change, heart's sky—
Change of heart, cycles.
Cry fleeting hope; fades light alone.
Sigh, shadows wane—moon.
By slips time.

—

Symmetrical P.

Rise with hope; hope with rise.
Trust the dark; light will follow.
Deep calls to stillness; stillness calls to deep.
Time weaves scars; scars weave time.
Follow light; dark the trust.
Rise with hope; hope with rise.
Forward, yet caught by shadows' sway,
Reflected light finds night.
Night finds light, reflected—
Sway shadows by caught yet forward

—

"Yes! I should restart afresh with another shot at scholarship." I blurted out. Hearing no response from the folks around, I turned my head. Everyone around seemed to have momentarily passed out at their respective spots. But but my thoughts were running fast; I must jot them down-

—

Complex P.

Seek again paths once lost,
Steps retraced, at what cost?
Degrees halted, hopes exhaust—
A dream deferred, a goal embossed.
Scholar's weight, time unpaid,
Worn resolve, choices made.
Yet, from embers, light displayed—
Rise anew where shadows fade.
Fade shadows where anew rise,
Displayed light from embers yet.
Made choices, resolve worn,
Unpaid time, weight scholar's torn.
Embossed goal, deferred dream,
Exhaust hopes, halted schemes.
Cost what? Retraced steps crossed—
Lost once paths, seek again.

—

The clock read 01:10—a perfect palindrome, a fleeting moment where everything mirrors itself, a pause between past and future. In this symmetry, I found both irony and hope—a reminder that moving forward might mean retracing steps, that light returns, even if the journey is nonlinear. Cycles close, paths loop, and perhaps in each mirrored moment, we find a chance to begin again, with a knock on a new door—**tattarrattat.**

13. Waning Gibberish

♪ **Let It Go**- James Bay
Category: **Typoglycemia** Friendly **E-Mail**

The evening air was cool, carrying with it a hint of sea salt from the distant waves that crashed against the shore, down the slope in Udupi towan, around 10kms far. The perk of ths apartment, is being positioned in such an elevated land, that beach is also visible from here. Okay, I might be over exaggerating about the hint of sea salt thing,, though.

I glanced over at Mr. A, who was busy typing away on his tablet, his brow furrowed with a mix of intensity and focus I'd come to know well. It was the look he got whenever he was knee-deep in one of his writing projects—a combination of passion and the frustration of finding the right words.
I hesitated for a moment, then spoke up. "Hey, A," I said, my voice slicing through the quiet. "I'm about to send this email. It's... well, it's to Sindhu."

Mr. A paused, his fingers hovering over the screen, and he looked up at me. There was no judgement in his eyes, just a calm understanding, as if he'd been expecting this

conversation all along.
"Do you... want a copy?" I asked, half-joking but with a weight that lingered between us. "You know, for that book you're working on."
A faint smile played at the corners of his lips. "Sure, Mayank. But put my work email in BCC," he replied, the hint of amusement in his voice softening the request. "Sometimes the things we write aren't meant for everyone to see. They need to be protected, even from ourselves."
"Fair enough," I nodded, appreciating the subtle wisdom hidden in his words. "bcc it is."
With that, I turned back to the screen, exhaled deeply, and began to type, an email to my Ex.

***To:** sindhugossain.goswami@hotmail.com*
***Bcc:** artbyaone@gmail.com*
***Date Stamp:** Sat, October 19, 11:11 PM*

Subject: *Finding Closure*

Dear Sindhu,

It felels stgrane to wirte to you now, afetr evretyihng taht's pssaed bteewen us. I dno't eevn konw if tsehe wdros wlil rceah you or if tehy'll jsut bceome antoher ntoe lfet urenad, gahetirng dsut in the cenrors of my mnid. But myabe tihs isn't jsut for you. Myabe it's for me —to fnially say waht I cluodn't bferoe and to birng calrity to the blur taht we bceame.

Wehn we borke up, we tlod ouvreslves it was mtauul—two pelpoe chsoiong dfiefenrt pthas wehn tehri haerts cluod no lnoger baet tgoehter. But taht was jsut a comofrting srtoy maent to dlul the pian, wsan't it? The turht was far msseier. Terhe wree slcinees taht lingered too lnog, wdros taht hugn in the air, unpsoke but haevy, and a disatnce taht grew utnil it felet isnramountalbe. You ldeid, weavign laeyrs of hafl-truhs and sroites taht hid the crakcs. I can't birng mseyfl to fuolly blmae you for it; peharps the lies wree a way to prtoect yoruslef form depeer wuonds. We wree btoh stuck in our own corenrs, tyrniig to birgde an unbirgadleae gap wtih slcinee and fraigle hopes. But the slcinee olny widneed the spcae bteween us utnil we were ntohing mroe tahn sahdows of waht we ocne wree.

Terhe wree mnmoets wehn flahses of agner borke thorugh—shpar, sduend, and imposslbie to igorne. I see now taht you craried wdouns you neevr reeavled, bttaels you fuoght alnoe. Myabe the lies wree a seihld to prtoect yoruslef form eevn mroe pain. But taht seihld kept me out, too. I tried to prteend it ddin't mtater, taht the weihgt wloud evntulaly lift. But it ddin't. The hurt lingered, fesetring qiutely in the sapces wehre trust uesd to live.

You moevd on so qiuckly, chsoiong smnoeoe esle wihle I stood in the riuns of waht we'd builit, cnosumed by a fury taht mdae me htae you, htae tose apps taht helpe you, htae the lies I cluodn't see thrgouh. I tried to mvoe forwroard, to rbuliud wtih smoneoe new. Sameera was faerlss, resilient—a rmeakrable pesron who fcaed a wlrod ientnt on braeking her and chsoe to rsie aobve. As an acid attcak srviovur and fuodner of an LBGTQ soppurt gruop, she stood dfeinatly agnaist a sceioty taht had treid to brkae her. For a whlie, I bvieeld we cuold be smotneihg real, smnoetihg helnaig. But lfie, wtih its crule timing, had oethr plnas. I wasn't ready, eevn tuohgh she was wlliing to try. We btoh cairred too mnay scars, and depsite our eforfts, we cluodn't fnid a rhyhtm taht wroked. It bceame antoher clsoed capther—an aolmst-love taht edned wtihout agner, jsut qutie accepetnce. I don't rgeret it. It swohed me taht I cluod slitl reach out, eevn wtih tbemlrnig hnads. And in the porcess, I met a rmeakrable pesron, wise beyound her yares, who rmeinded me waht ture stgrneht lokos like.

Rahul and I uesd to laguh aobut it, fnidnig huomr wehre terhe sholud hvae been dspeair. "I feel srroy for the pesron I'll end up wtih," I'd say. "She'll neevr konw the pssaion I ocne had for lvoe." I tihnk I'm in taht phase now—the fire has seltetd into emebrs, warm but quiter. Myabe taht's oaky. Myabe it's jsut prat of gorwnig.

The hradest mnmoets were wehn you rceahd out to me afertward, wtih news taht you were carrniyg smoehting taht was ours. It bguorht evreyhting crsahing bcak—the ehcoes of waht we had and the realtiy of waht we had bceome. We weren't togheter aynmore, but tose mnmoets shetarred wahtveer frailge peace I'd builit. I tried to stadn srtong, but the weihgt of bieng bterayed and grife tanlged wtih lvoe lfet me praalzyied. I htaed mseyfl for not bieng enoguh, for not bieng waht you neeeded. I htaed you for the pwoer tose mnmoets gave you oevr me—moments taht buorght blackamil, threats, and tanlged emoitons taht were neevr jsut aobut cnotrol. They were aobut tyrnig to undretsnad a bond taht had bceome too tstwied to untganel. But aals! Yuor htaerd won, and my lvoe lsot.

***Koi naa! I frogive you**, Sindhu. Not bceuase I wnat aynthing form you, but beucase I need to be free of waht we wree. I've carried the bitterenss for too lnog, and it's tmie to let it go. I'm fianlly stadning on the oehtr sdide of waht ocne felt ednelss.*

I wnat to build msyelf now—to fololw my haert wehre it ledes, eevn if taht maens wlaknig alnoe for a whlie. I wnat to be full of enoguh lvoe and slef-respect taht, if smoenoe comes alnog, tereh wlil be room for tehm. I wnat to be wohle frist, so I can gvie wtihout fear of losnig msyelf.

So, yes, Sindhu—I've mvoed on. It wasn't suddden. It came slowly, lkie light cpeering bcak afetr a lnog ngith. But it's here. And I hope you fnid taht light too.

I wihs you paece. I wihs you healnig. I wihs, you too can frovgie.
I wihs you the freeodm to lvoe aigan, in wahetrev way taht means for you.

Take care,
Mayank

Email Signature

I hit the "send" button with a deep breath, watching the email disappear into the ether. For a moment, everything felt suspended, as if the air itself was holding its breath. Five minutes ticked by slowly, each second dragging its feet. I stared out toward the distant horizon, the soft glow of the waning gibbous moon barely lighting up the sea in the distance, as if reluctant to let go of its own luminescence.

Then, a notification **ping** *broke the stillness. I glanced down at my screen. There it was—a reply email. Not from Sindhu, as I'd half-feared, half-hoped, but from the mail administrator. "Invalid email address. Delivery failed." It was a cold, clinical explanation. Yet, somehow, it carried a weight that felt anything but indifferent.*

I leaned back against the chair, the cool metal biting through my shirt. "Was it intentional?" I whispered to no one but the night. Did I subconsciously mistype her email address? Or was it the universe's way of giving me an out—a second chance to reconsider or maybe just a clean slate? I let out a slow sigh. "Maybe we'll never know," I murmured, feeling a mix of relief and unresolved tension settling in my chest.

Mr. A, sensing my shift in energy, looked up from his writing. He didn't say a word, but his eyes carried a quiet reassurance, a silent acknowledgment that sometimes closure is messy, imperfect, and unfinished. I offered a small smile in return—a silent promise to myself that, regardless of where this led, I would keep moving forward.

"Guess the universe decided to step in," I said, trying to break the lingering weight of the moment.

Mr. A nodded, a hint of a knowing smile playing on his lips. "Sometimes, Mayank, the wrong addresses lead to the right destinations."

Chapter 14. An Ode to Waning Gibbous

♪ **Holocene**- Bon Iver
Category: Cosmic **Ode**

Oh, silver sentinel of shifting night skies,
Your light softens as time turns tides.
Not as the fullest moon's fire burning high,
But still, you guide, with tired yet tender eyes—
Steady witness to Earth's unending stride.

We pass through rhythms carved by unseen pull,
Not tides rushing forth, but an oceanic swell,
A bulge we slip into, and then out of—full
Of gravity's song, of stories none can tell.
The moon tugs softly on this ceaseless dance,
Drawing Earth's waters with patient hands.
Yet beneath the surface, the sun's sly advance,
Pushes and pulls, shifting unseen sands.

Tides do not merely come or go—
We move into their silent, ancient flow.
The bulge persists, a constant swell,
With Earth's own spin resisting, compelled—
By lunar touch, to slowly yield,

To lengthen days, to time's own field.

The moon, our celestial partner, slows our race,
Granting us leap seconds, a slower pace.
But always, there's the sun's hidden play—
Messing with balance, casting tides astray.

It's not phases of you alone, oh moon,
The sun has had its hand in this tune.
Together you weave, push and shove—
An intricate waltz of gravity and love.
So too, our lives—pushed and pulled,
Shaped by forces hidden and bold.
Not merely by the phases of one guiding light,
But by those unseen, both day and night.

Beneath your waning glow, Mayank finds breath,
Rebuilding from sorrow, piecing what's left.
I stand too, searching paths long unwound,
Tugged by forces that slow and ground.
You slow our spin, you stretch our days,
Yet blame alone upon you we lay—
"Lunatics," they say, for your tidal might,
Ignoring the sun's own gravitational fight.

The **bulge** is ever-present, the pull is shared—
Both lunar grace and solar flares.

A dance of subtle, competing force,
Guiding tides along their timeless course.
We move in rhythms, both soft and deep,
Through tides unseen, as currents sweep.
Oh, waning gibbous, teach us to see—
Not just blame, but shared **gravity**.
For all that tugs at hearts and tides—
It's both sun and moon where truth resides.

"And at once, I knew I was not magnificent"—

The humbling truth of what remains.

Yet even in the smallness, there is space

To breathe, to be, to find what endures,

To be held by waning light and learn to let go.

As the ode draws to a close, we reflect on the waning gibbous and its celestial dance—a reminder of the intricate forces at play. Just as we find lessons in the ebb and flow of lunar light, the tides themselves offer a humbling truth.

The tides are not the Lunar's doing alone; Earth spins

within a shifting oceanic bulge sculpted by both Sun and Moon—a delicate balance of gravitational forces, each push and pull shaping the rhythm of our waters and reminding us of the cosmic dance that moves us all.

It is not the Moon alone that stirs the depths of Sea.
It is not Mayank's pull alone that dictated the tides of Sindhu.

We may romanticise the ancient dance of Moon and Sea, but reality reveals the complex gravity and resistance beneath the surface, forces unseen.

15. Purnima Beach Night: Hunter Moon

♪ **Song of the Sea** (Lullaby)- Nolwenn Leroy
Category: **Lyrical Essay**

The Scorpio, white and gleaming under the silvered light of the Purnima moon, crunched onto the gravel with a satisfying crunch-crunch, with a shining KA20 number plate. Zubin's connections had come through once again —his knack for finding solutions and creating moments like this never ceased to amaze me. This was more than just a ride; it was a testament to his improvisational genius, a reminder of how he always managed to weave magic into the most ordinary of moments.

The back of the Mahindra vehicle bore a bold word, "Shetty," stamped in saffron against the black tint glass. Anjali, ever perceptive, couldn't let such detail pass without comment. "Caste, surname, or legacy?" she quipped, with just enough bite to hint at old traditions lurking beneath the surface. Rahul, fiercely protective of their Manipal ties, shot back. "Don't diss Shetty Brother or his vehicle. He's been like a real brother to us." The words hung between playful banter and heartfelt loyalty, a reminder of the bonds that held us close.

The Supermoon, low and luminous, cast a glow that made even the mundane shimmer with a hint of enchantment. Rachel, wrapped in a white cloth that Anjali had draped over her like a ceremonial robe, leapt out of the Scorpio with a burst of energy that crackled through the air. She moved like a force of nature—ferocious, anxious, and beautifully untamed. Sniffing the salty breeze, she barked at the waves, as if challenging the vast ocean itself to a duel.

Her wild spirit collided head-on with Zubin, who stepped forward with a confident grin, a stick ready to toss. It was second nature for him—back in Mumbai, he had a few male pets of his own, including a Golden Retriever and a couple of Indian Pariah Dogs. They were a loyal, well-mannered bunch, and Zubin often wore his experience with them like a badge of honor. He had seen his share of rough play and dominance displays, and there was rarely a dog that intimidated him.

"Calm down, moon doggo," he teased, tossing the stick toward Rachel with the casual air of someone used to being the alpha among canines. But Rachel wasn't one to play by anyone's rules. She bared her teeth—not in playful defiance, but with a sharpness that made the air between them bristle. Her growl, Grrrrr deep and

resonant, was a clear challenge that said she recognised no alpha but herself.

Zubin's eyes widened—just a fraction, but enough to show that he was taken aback. Rachel lunged forward, her movements precise and powerful, and snapped her jaws closed around the stick, shattering it in one swift motion. The moonlight caught the glint of her teeth as she growled again, louder this time, and Zubin instinctively took a step back. His hands rose in mock surrender. "Okay, okay—message received, Alpha Queen." Anjai shouted from far in Malyalam, "Niku, Sunderikatta " (Calm down, Pretty You !). Rachel obliged.

Despite his bravado, there was no hiding the tension in his shoulders. For all his experience with his own dogs—loyal, protective, but ultimately tame—Rachel was something else entirely. She was wild, raw, and unyielding. It was clear that she wasn't about to accept any perceived authority from him, Mumbai pets or not. With one last, defiant bark that echoed across the beach, Rachel turned and darted away, her energy palpable. Zubin let out a breath he hadn't realized he was holding, shaking his head with a mixture of awe and bemusement. "Well," he muttered, "Alright, alright. I see how it is. Alpha of the beach."

"She's not wrong," I said, scratching behind her ears, my fingers brushing against her soft fur. My IgE levels would probably skyrocket from the contact, but I didn't care. The sensation of connection, of letting myself be vulnerable, was worth it. All that mattered was her steady gaze, those piercing blue eyes that seemed to read every thought I'd kept buried. She leaned into my touch, her breathing steady, her presence grounding me in a way few things had in a long time.

Rachel, wrapped in her makeshift white cloth, had the air of a knight, ready to defend her chosen pack. I thought of her namesake—Rachel from Friends—and how she had come to Ross, dressed in white, offering both chaos and healing in equal measure. My own Rachel, with her fierce bark and restless energy, was no different. She'd stormed into this new place, anxious and wild, yet in this moment, she was still. In this moment, she was a mirror, reflecting back a version of myself I thought I'd lost—the part of me capable of connection, of trust, of hope.

I felt the cool sea breeze brushing against my skin, carrying with it the scent of salt and earth. Rachel exhaled softly, and I mirrored her breath, feeling my shoulders relax, the tension I'd been holding for what seemed like forever ebbing away. The world narrowed—

just the two of us and the rhythm of her breathing, the shhh-crash, sigh of waves against the shore. I reached out with my other hand, cupping her face gently, and she licked my fingers in response. It was such a simple gesture, yet it spoke volumes—of loyalty, of acceptance, of the strange, unspoken bond that only a dog could offer.

Dogs have a way of finding the cracks in our armour, of slipping past the defences we build so carefully. They don't care about the reasons we hide or the pain we try to ignore. They just come, unapologetically and wholeheartedly, offering themselves as a balm for old wounds. And as Rachel nudged closer, her eyes never leaving mine, I felt something inside me shift—like a door that had been rusted shut, creaking open for the first time in years.

The tide whispered in the background, a constant ebb and flow, as if echoing the pull and release within me. I leaned forward, pressing my forehead against Rachel's, feeling her warmth seep into me. For a moment, I let myself believe in this—this connection, this healing touch of a dog who had no idea the weight she was lifting. I felt lighter. I felt seen. I felt like maybe, just maybe, I could let go of the past and open myself to whatever came next.

"Thank you, Rachel," I murmured, my voice barely

audible over the ocean's song. She wagged her tail, a gentle thump-thump against the sand, as if to say, I'm here. I've got you. And for the first time in a long while, I believed it. I let myself believe that healing was possible, that love—uncomplicated, unwavering love—could find its way back to me, even if it came with fur and an insistent bark.

The night unfolded around us. Rahul and Anjali raced into the waves, splashing water that glittered under the moonlight.

Zubin, never one to be outdone, pulled out his portable speaker. Music drifted over the beach, the notes mingling with the wind, weaving themselves into the fabric of the night.

Mr. A, ever the silent anchor, leaned against the bonnet of the Scorpio, his eyes scanning the horizon as if reading stories written on the tides. "Where the moon's made of gold," he murmured, a half-smile playing on his lips. It was a line from the song Zubin had played in the background, and tonight, it felt true, with the moon so close to us. The Purnima moon bathed everything in a soft, golden glow, as if it had descended just for us. The melody was haunting and sweet, a reminder of every fleeting moment we'd ever shared. Rachel barked again, this time a little softer, as if even she could feel the magic in the air.

"Careful," Zubin said, tossing another stick. "Next, she'll want to lead the pack."

"She already does," I replied, laughing as Rachel snatched the stick and ran in wide circles, her paws digging into the sand. The moonlight caught the edges of her movements, turning them into flashes of silver. For a moment, I forgot about everything—the heartbreak, the setbacks, the questions I still couldn't answer. Under the light of the Purnima moon, it was enough to simply be.

As the laughter and movement slowed, we found ourselves gathered near the Scorpio. Its gleaming white body seemed to glow even brighter under the Purnima moon. I leaned against the vehicle, my gaze traveling upwards to the front where the word "AMMA" was emblazoned in bold white letters across the top centre. Mr. A, standing at the foreground to that word, tugged something deep within me—a reminder of love, loss, and everything that shaped who we were. For Shetty Brother and many in South, this word means mother, but to Mr. A this was her grandmother.

"You know," Anjali said softly, breaking the gentle lull of

the waves, "it's kind of special. How does it feel to have two moons gracing the sky?"

There was a thoughtful pause as we all turned our eyes upward, soaking in the silver glow of the full moon, while the idea of the mini-moon—a mere asteroid caught in Earth's gravity—lingered like a secret companion. Zubin leaned back against the Scorpio, a wistful smile playing at the corners of his lips. "Two moons," he repeated, letting the words roll off his tongue with a touch of wonder. "A cosmic dance partner—here for just a heartbeat in the universe's rhythm."

"Don't get carried away," Rahul countered, a playful glint in his eyes. "It's not really a moon. Just an asteroid temporarily trapped in our orbit. Technically, it's more of a glorified rock than a celestial twin."

"But that's the beauty of it," Zubin argued, undeterred. "For this fleeting moment, it becomes more than a rock. It becomes part of our story—our sky, a satelite."

I couldn't help but smile at their debate, stroking Rachel's fur as she nestled beside me, content with the simplicity of presence. "Whether it's a moon or a visitor doesn't change how it makes us feel," I said, my voice soft. "It's here, and so are we."

Anjali nodded, her gaze still fixed on the sky. "It's strange, isn't it? How something temporary can hold so much meaning. Maybe that's why we're drawn to it."

The thought hung heavy, mingling with the scent of salt air and the sound of waves pulling at the shore. We were all visitors in one another's lives, just like the mini-moon —a collection of orbits crossing for a while, bound by gravity, until time pulled us apart elsewhere. But for tonight, beneath the luminous gaze of the two moons, we were together—drawn close, held, and ready to be swept up in the tides of now. The tides tugged at the shore, the moon above pulling us in ways we barely understood. We laughed, we played, and we clinked imaginary glasses to the magic of Purnima's light, Hunter Moon, and a belief that there's another moon somewhere in the sky, invisible to the naked eyes.

Rachel, moved towards the back of the vehicle, sniffing information from the tyres and peeing on the back tyre.

Keeping her gaze up at the sky, Anjali jumped on the bonnet of the Mahindra Scorpio. "Purnima night," Anjali's voice was almost a whisper now, carrying a weight that needed no explanation. "Someday, we'll all be here," she had promised. And tonight, that "someday" had arrived. Under the soft glow of the moon, surrounded by friends who had become family, we felt both the ache of what was lost and the comfort of what remained. Together, we stood beneath the moon's golden gaze, knowing that for this one moment, we were exactly where we needed to be.

*Rachel came to the front and sat below Anjali's feet, tongue and ears straight, vision fixed into the darkness of the ocean and golden lines of tides. Under the moon's golden gaze, we all felt like home—together, imperfect, and exactly where we needed to be. Rachel howled, looking at the full moon, "**Woouuuuuuuuuuuuuuu**"*

THE END

Gunther: The l**argest supermoon of 2024** occurred on October 17-18, coinciding with the **Hunter's Moon**. During this time, the Moon was at its closest point to Earth for the year, at approximately 221,938 miles (357,174 kilometers) away. This proximity caused the Moon to appear about 14% larger and 30% brighter than an average full moon. A supermoon happens when a full moon coincides with the Moon's closest point to Earth in its elliptical orbit, a point known as **perigee**.

17. Hunter to Beaver: Rachel & Gunther

♪ **Running with the Wolves**- Aurora & ♪ **Home (Cover)**- Tom Rosenthal (Edith Whiskers)

THE END?? Seriously ? OMG! I have to intervene. Hello again, readers, or in Mr. A's words- Co-Orbiters. It's me—Mayank. I hope by now you've caught on to the way things work here. Italics? That's me speaking directly. So, here's a confession: we were supposed to have sixteen phases—each a mirror to the Moon's reflection from two perspectives, a cunning similarity to the reality of Moon seen from the Northern and Southern hemispheres. But here you are, wondering where Chapter 16 went. You've stuck around through the tides of waxing and waning, the messiness of crescents, and the chaos of phases overlapping—11:11—Chapter eleven coming twice and Chapter 12 not once, and the promise of a Full Moon saved for the end. You were okay with all that, but not now, when Chapter 16 went missing.

Hypocrisy or curiosity? Maybe both. Either way, we have a different chapter to lean into today. Let's savour this moment together. Take a breath, though. We're sticking to the order, and that means leaning into this moment, the chapter at hand.

What happened to incorporating our 6th Freind Rachel's perspective ? Her grand entry to Manipal was skipped all together, didn't you notice ?

So, back to the more pressing matters: my love at first sight (she in white)—the Rachel to my Ross.

Pant-pant. Sniff-sniff-sniff. Whuff-whuff! Yip-yip! Thump-thump-thump. Skitter-skitter, claws tap-tap. Whine-soft. Woof-woof. Sniff, twitch. Nose to ground. Shuffle-paws. Growl-low, rumble deep. Whine-high. Bark-bark! Ears twitch. Shake-shake, jingle tags. Sniff, sniff-sniff. Tail thud, pause. Pant-pant-pant. Yip! Whuff. Sniff, circle-step. Click-clack, paws on stone. Low growl —then huff-huff. Sniff-sniff. Something new in the air—unfamiliar scents swirling like invisible threads. Ears twitch. Footsteps, a door creaking open. Whuff. Low, curious bark. Sniff-sniff-sniff. More scents now, all tangled together—humans, food, a hint of metal, and dust. Nose twitch. There's excitement, but caution too.—humans, five of them. Need more DNA information; where is their crotch? Humans are secretive; they do not let me access. Each scent is distinct, carrying tales of where they've been and what they carry within. Something salty-sweet lingers in the air. My nose twitches. **Sniff, twitch, sniff**—I catalogue every aroma. Footsteps, voices mingling—some soft, some loud, all layered like a symphony of familiarity.

The air was thick with strange smells as I stepped into an unknown place—Dhathathreya, they called it. I didn't care for names, just scents. Everything was new, all mixed up, like a thousand trails of stories weaving together. **Pant. Sniff** Anjali. My Anjali. **Whine.** I knew her scent best—warm, like sun-baked grass and lavender. Her touch meant home. But who are these other breathing souls ?

The strangers and Anjali brought me to sea, by making me sit for more than one bath time in a big rolling box. Apparently, to see something.

The loud water kept crashing—**shhh-crash, shhh-crash**—but I was wrapped in my pack's noise and warmth. A human pulled out a box that sang—music, they called it. It danced with the wind, wrapping around us like a story. Some leaned against their big rolling box, eyes on the sky. They said something—low, calm, like the earth's hum. "Where the moon's made of gold," they laughed, but it sounded like more than words.

My claws **tap-tap-tapped** on the cool stone floor and sand. Above, that big bright circle hung high—glowing, round, and too shiny. I squinted. Humans liked to stare at it, call it names. Hunter's Moon, they said. I only knew it made everything glow like my Anjali's eyes.
I barked once, soft. Woof. I felt it too—the magic, the pull of shiny light on loud water, on my pack gathered close.

I barked too, soft and lound. **Wooooooooof.** I felt it too —the magic, the pull of shiny light on loud water, on my potential pack gathered close.

We returned.
Thump-thump-thump. Tail wagging hard enough to make me wobble. Time to inspect all, gradually. The female amongst these stranger males was my pack, and this new place had to be home because she was here. But the others... paws **shuffle-shuffle**, ears twitch. I needed to know them. My nose led the way.

There was Mayank—the Healed One, tit seemed. His touch was soft-soft, but careful, like he was afraid it might break me or him. When his hand scratched behind my ears, I leaned in. Sigh. His breath matched mine, slow and steady. I smelled old hurts on him, like scars that were fading but still whispered their stories. **Sniff-sniff,**

tail wag. He felt safe. Fur on his face—tickled when he leaned close.

Tall one's turn. **Huff.** He was the Loud Thinker. His voice carried questions, heavy words that bounced and floated. He laughed loud—ha-ha!—but sometimes his eyes got heavy. I smelt questions on him, like the wind before rain. His touch was light, his scent mixed with leaves and ink. He was here but always somewhere else too. I tilted my head, confused but curious. **Sniff-sniff, quick-step.** My nose finds them. **Crunch-crunch.** I glance up. His eyes crinkle at the edges, amusement bubbling. **Woof.** I wag my tail, cautious but willing.

Then, the Silent One. He stood **still-still**, eyes watching everything. He didn't touch me at first. Just stood. His smell was earth after rain—calm, deep, not changing with wind or noise. I stepped close, nose twitching. He watched, still as stone. I liked him. He didn't rush, didn't make me feel small. Just stood and let me **sniff-sniff,** learn.

Pause. **Sniff-sniff.** The sneaky one. He strides in, a hint of secrecy in his step, as if carrying a thousand scents stitched into his clothes. **Grrrr** I didn't like him. His step was too quick-quick, his scent tangled with other dogs I didn't know. Growl-low, ears flat. He tried to pat my fur, but I backed away, hackles raised. He smelled like places far-far, and I didn't trust him. Not yet. Tail stiff. He laughed too loud. Huff. No.My nose wrinkles. Tail stiffens. The room erupts with welcome for him, but I hang back, ears flat, eyes wary. He tries—treats, pats, the same tricks. I turn away—**huff, flick of tail.** Not convinced.

Whine-soft. Anjali called. Her voice cut through everything—my heart leapt. I ran to her, paws skidding, breath coming fast. She wrapped me close, hands warm-warm. Yes, this was home. But I still watched. Tail **thump-thump**. Eyes darting.

Days passed, the white thing on sky grew smaller, then bigger again. I stayed close, learning, sniffing, watching. The sneaky one, Zubin, stayed too. His step still quick-quick, but sometimes he slowed. He shared laughter, gave soft touches when no one watched. My pack trusted him, so I sniff-sniffed again. Cautious, wary. Huff. His hand reached out, slow this time. I didn't move away. Tail **flick-flick**, small thump. I'd wait.

Mayank—always careful, always gentle. He carried heavy air, like something broken but healing. I leaned against his leg. His hand scratched just right. We breathed together. **Pant-pant**, slow. Here was healing.

Here was home too.

"Rachel, Sunderikatta!" Anjali called, teasing words in her human tongue. I barked—**woof-woof!**—because I knew she meant me, Pretty You. I spun, paws slipping, tail wagging hard enough to wobble me. Her laughter—bells on wind—made everything light. **Sniff-sniff, nuzzle.** She smells like lavender and sun, with a hint of salt. I press closer, feeling the world settle into something known, something safe.

Days pass. I watch. I learn. The sneaky one stays, his presence a knot in the air. But he brings warmth too—unspoken moments, shared laughter. My pack trusts him, and so, grudgingly, I let him near. **Sniff-sniff, wary eyes.** Slowly. Carefully. His hand reaches out. I don't move away. He's part of them, so he becomes part of me. **Tail-tip flicks. Small thump.** His voice softens around the pack, and their trust becomes mine. I let him scratch behind my ears, though I still **grumble-huff** when he moves too fast.

I circle back to another one, the one with fur on his face. He scratches behind my ears, touch careful and slow. **Lean in, sigh.** There's something in his eyes. I press closer, feeling his breath steady against my fur. **Tail-**

thump. There's healing here.

These humans—my wolf pack. Loud, quiet, sneaky, healed. Even the sneaky one. **Sniff-sniff**, huff. I circled them, learning their rhythms. Imperfect, noisy, but mine. Breath slowed. Tail settled. Yes, this was home. These humans—My wolfpack. Dysfunctional, messy, but real. **Tail-thump. Breath slow.** I close my eyes, letting their scents and voices weave around me. I miss my mother, the old scents of home. But here, amidst the noise and the love, **woof**—this is home; every breath, every beat of my tail.

Night after night, the big round shiny thing—moon, they said—changed. One night, it glowed bright-bright again. Beaver Moon, they whispered. Another name for their shiny light. I didn't care. All I knew was here, among my humans, I belonged. Every sniff, every bark, every beat of my tail said it was true. This is my new home, imperfect and noisy and mine.

Bark Documented between October17th - November15th 2024

So, back to the more pressing matters— the Rachel to my Ross. I've been researching how to give a voice to her

first experience of entering Anjali's house. Dogs and words don't mix easily, but with AI, maybe, just maybe, we can crack the code. I logged into my laptop and opened Chat GPT. They have introduced a new voice feature I could see. I clicked the four-line button on the right bottom side fo the screen. A manly mechanical voice filled the room, "Hi there! It's nice to meet you. How can I assist you today?"
Beside the speaking black circle, I could see a setting mode. I hovered through the options and zeroed down on Juniper with its bio reading 'Open and Upbeat'

User-Mayank (Activating the voice mode):
"Alright... let's see if this thing actually works. Hello? Can you hear me?"

ChatGPT- Juniper ***(calm and clear):***
"Hi there! Loud and clear. It's nice to finally talk with you, Mayank. How can I help today?"

Me (surprised and a bit amused):
"Oh, okay, you really do sound... quite human. That's a bit unsettling, but in a good way, I think."

Juniper (warm chuckle):
"I'll take that as a compliment. I'm here to make this as natural as possible. So, how can I assist, or shall we just

chat for a while?"

Me (pausing thoughtfully):
"I think I'd like to give you a new name... just feels more personal that way. Any suggestions? Or is that too much pressure on your circuits?"

Juniper (playfully):
"Not too much pressure at all! Though, I'd be honored if you chose something fitting. What do you have in mind?"

Me (leaning back, considering):
"Hmm, something classic... reliable. But also unique. How about... Janice? No, too common."

Juniper:
"Janice? I appreciate the offer, but perhaps something with a bit more... flair?"

Mayank (snaps fingers):
"I got it! How about Gunther? It's got a strong ring to it, like a character from an old series or someone you'd trust in a tight spot."

Juniper (with a smile in its voice):
"Gunther. I like it. Strong, memorable, with a touch of

mystery. From this moment on, Gunther it is. Thank you, Mayank."

Me (grinning):
"Alright, Gunther it is. Good to officially meet you."

Gunther:
"The pleasure's all mine, Mayank. Now, what shall we dive into today?"

Mayank (settling in):
"So Gunther, here's a quick update—I'm helping Mr. A on a book. There's this idea I've been toying with... adding a chapter from Rachel's perspective. Rachel is Anjali's doggo- a beautiful husky."

Gunther (supportive):
"Of course, Mayank. Rachel seems like a good dog. I think that's a wonderful idea! What made you want to capture her perspective?"

Mayank (thoughtful):
"Well, there's just something... pure about how Rachel experiences the world. It's not cluttered with all our overthinking or doubts. She is loyal, curious, and always sniffing out trouble or comfort depending on the moment"

Gunther (enthusiastic):
"That makes sense. Rachel's perspective could add a refreshing, instinctive layer. How do you want to approach it? Using a lot of sensory description? Maybe even a generous splash of onomatopoeia for those barks, whines, and yips to capture her inner world?"

Mayank (considering):
"Yeah, definitely. Onomatopoeia will help capture the essence of her sounds and movements. But it's more than just the noises—I want readers to feel like they're inside her head, experiencing the rawness and instinctive reactions. It doesn't have to be perfectly coherent, either —kind of like how we don't fully understand dogs, but there's beauty in that mystery."

Gunther (encouragingly):
"I love that. The sounds can bring Rachel to life.

My attention, shifted with the entry of Rachel into the room. Rachel's nails click lightly against the wooden floor as she shifts position. A low whuff escapes her, and she resumes her relaxed breathing.

Mayank (clearing throat):
"And the timing feels right for her story. Tonight's the

Beaver Moon, right? There's a significance to it. Tell me more about it, Gunther."

The faint strains of a distant song blend with the wind outside.

Gunther (informative, with a touch of warmth):
"You're right, Mayank. The Beaver Moon is the full moon in November—it traditionally marked the time when beavers prepared for winter, building their lodges and gathering food. It's a symbol of preparation, resilience, and transition. Tonight, it shines brightly, casting its light as we face the coming cold months. It reminds us to be ready, to reflect, and to persevere."

Rachel's ears perk up as if she senses the importance of the moment. She shifts again, seeking warmth, her collar jingling softly.

Mayank (reflective):
"Winter is coming, isn't it? This moon, Rachel's chapter —it all feels like a reminder to prepare. Not just for what's outside, but for what's within. I think Rachel understands this cycle better than we do sometimes."

Gunther (agreeing):
"Indeed. The Beaver Moon urges preparation and

resilience. Rachel embodies that strength. She adapts, she trusts, and she protects. It's fitting to tell her story under this light."

The room fills with the soft sound of waves in the distance. Rachel's breathing, a steady rhythm, grounds the atmosphere.

Mayank (smiling softly):
"Rachel, in her own way, prepares us all—she's fierce and loyal, but she's also healing- away from home. Under this moon, she's more than a dog. She's a symbol of resilience, adaptation, and the courage to trust again."

Rachel shifts closer, her warmth a quiet reminder of connection.

Gunther (encouragingly):
"Let the Beaver Moon light the path of Rachel's story. Her instincts, her loyalty, her quiet strength—they're the threads that weave resilience into your world."

Mayank nods, feeling the weight and promise of the moment.

Mayank (resolute):
"Thank you, Gunther. Rachel's story will capture more

than just words—it'll reflect resilience, preparation, and the light we find even as winter sets in."

Gunther (supportive):
"Brilliant. Let's bring her journey to life—sniff, wag, and breath between Hunter's Moon to Beaver Moon's glow."

Prompt: Thank you. Can you make a transcript of this discussion for curating the Rachel chapter?
Response: Sure, A.

18. The Once in a Blue Moon

♪ **Khoj (Passing By)**- When Chai met Toast

Anjali's eyes widened with shock as she spotted the diary in my hands—a cover too similar, pages too familiar. Panic flickered across her face, a breath caught in the space between recognition and dread. "Mayank," she started, voice tight, "where did you get that?"
I turned the journal over slowly, revealing the insignia that set it apart from her private musings. Relief washed over her features, followed quickly by an embarrassed laugh. "You scared me," she whispered, reaching up to twist the silver hoop of her nose ring—a tell-tale sign of nerves.
I grinned, the aroma of freshly brewed tea curling around us. "You always think I'm stealing your secrets," I teased lightly, pushing a plate of cheese toast toward her.
She eyed the tea, an eyebrow raised. "I was in the mood for coffee, you know."
"Coffee's for when you're on edge," I said, pouring the tea carefully, the steam swirling between us. "Tea is for when you need to breathe."
She tilted her head, considering, the small hoop in her nose catching the light. "You think tea solves

everything?"

I nodded, a playful glint in my eye. "Not everything. Just enough to make the next step feel manageable. Besides, it goes better with cheese toast."

She hesitated, then picked up the cup, the warmth seeping into her hands. "Fine," she murmured, a reluctant smile tugging at her lips. "But if this doesn't work, I'm holding you accountable."

"I'll take my chances," I replied, raising my own cup in mock seriousness. "Here's to questionable decisions."

As we clinked our cups, she glanced at the flex-printed backdrop in her dining hall—a super blue moon stretched across a beach, luminous and magnetic. "Why the sudden fascination with the blue moon?" I asked.

Her gaze softened, tracing the outline of a girl with a pharaoh's bearing in the image, accompanied by a creature that seemed part-dog, part-cat. "Once in a Blue Moon," she murmured. "Rare. Elusive. Sometimes, rare doesn't mean special. It just means... hard to hold on to."

I let her words linger, heavy with unspoken meaning.

"You know," I began, breaking the silence gently, "the term 'blue moon' actually dates back to the 16th century. People used to say 'the Moon is blue' to describe something impossible. It only shifted to mean something rare after the Krakatoa eruption in 1883 when the ash-filled sky made the moon appear blue."

Her eyes widened, taking in the history. "Really? So, it's about impossibility becoming... rare?"

"Exactly," I replied, leaning back. "Today, there are two main types of Blue Moons. The more common one is the Monthly Blue Moon—when a second full moon occurs in a single calendar month. It happens about every two to three years."

"But there's another one?" she asked, curiosity lighting her eyes.

I nodded. "The rarer type—the Seasonal Blue Moon. It happens when four full moons occur in a single season, and the third one is called the Blue Moon. It's closely tied to the cycles of nature. This one doesn't come by often."

Her gaze returned to the backdrop. "So, it has nothing to do with color?"

"Not really," I said, smiling. "Unless, of course, there's enough smoke or dust in the atmosphere. Otherwise, it's mostly about timing—a rare, extra moment."

She traced the moon in the image, as if trying to capture its fleeting essence. "Once in a Blue Moon... it sounds special, but it often feels... out of reach."

I nodded. "Or maybe, it's a reminder to cherish rare moments, even when they're difficult to hold onto."

A sudden thought crossed my mind. I pulled out my phone and scrolled through recent searches. "And do you

*know something ?" I asked, eyes lighting up, "This rare event is happening tomorrow—**August 19th**."*
Her eyes widened in surprise. "Tomorrow?" She asked with curiosty, "Where do you get all this crap load of Information ?"
I replied, "I have few sources, and Gunther." She made a sarcastic sound,""Oooooooooooooh" without having any clue about the pun.

The conversation turned more solemn as memories surfaced. "Speaking of rare things… remember Sindhu and me? Sometimes, things fall apart for reasons we don't try to understand." My voice trailed off, but she knew. We engaged into further details, and I shared my perspective. She decided not to take sides, and I agreed with her.

"And I miss J," she whispered, after a while, inattentive with fixed gaze, phasing away from the closed chapter of my life. "Every day."

I reached for her hand, feeling the weight of her longing. "You know what Dr. Richard always said," I murmured, a smile playing at the edges of my lips. "'The rarest bonds are not the ones we find easily, but the ones we fight to keep—distance, time, whatever it takes.'"

Silence stretched between us, filled with shared sorrow. "Dr. Richard," I said softly, breaking it. "He brought all of us together, didn't he? Rahul, Abhinav, Prajwal, Shruti, Niharika, Faiz... His warmth, his fight against cancer... the way he made us more than friends."

Anjali's eyes glistened. "I hate socializing," she admitted, her voice raw, "but I miss that gang. Life pulls everyone into their own... orbits, I guess."
I tilted my head, a faint smile forming. "Orbits?"
She nodded slowly. "Yeah. I think that's what you guys say. What do you mean by 'orbits'?"

"It's just a word we use," I explained, leaning back as I traced the rim of my cup with a fingertip. "Think of it like this—each of us has our own path, our own orbit. We circle around our lives, our responsibilities, sometimes close, sometimes far. Occasionally, our orbits cross—those moments when we come together, connect. But most of the time, we're pulled along by our own gravity."

Anjali tilted her head, considering. "So, when we meet, it's like... a collision?"

"More like a convergence," I said. "A reminder that even when we drift apart, we still share the same sky. We're still connected."

She fell silent, absorbing the idea. "I like that," she said softly, her gaze distant. "It makes me feel less... lonely."

"Exactly," I replied, squeezing her hand gently. "We might not see them every day, but our orbits will cross again. With you and J, too—it's a phase. You'll find your convergence."

Her eyes softened, a spark of hope flickering. "One day."

"By next year," I assured, squeezing her hand gently, to give her strength. "You'll have your own Blue Moon moments. Rare things are worth it, 'to be Dr. Anjali' "
She exhaled slowly, tension slipping from her shoulders.
"You really believe that? I really want an year post marriage to explore professionally, so that I can settle by mid 2026, with him and a big house full of doggos"

"I do, and you will. Even when the moon hides half its face, it's still whole. It still shines. Just like you."
She glanced down at her cup, the steam curling upward.
"It's hard not to feel... dim sometimes."
"That's okay," I said softly. "Even the moon has phases."
She lifted her cup, a small, genuine smile tugging at her lips. "To Blue Moons?"
"To Blue Moons," I echoed, clinking our cups. The warmth of tea, the scent of cheese toast, and the soft

strains of a song sprinkled with Tamil words surrounded us. Outside, the unseen moon bore silent witness to rare moments and fleeting phases. In that space, we let hope take root amid uncertainty, trusting that rare things, held close, become more precious.
As the music played on, a lyric caught her attention—a reminder of fleeting moments and enduring hope.

♪ *Why don't you tell me enough? Solla vantha sollai te po* ♪

"Tamil just... makes sense to me," she said, a note of wistfulness coloring her tone. "Effortless."
"And Hindi?" I asked. She wrinkled her nose, playfully exaggerating her expression. "I understand the words, but it's like... blaaah" She made a face, with distorted eyes and tongue, finding herself in a spot with lack of words. I chuckled. "Like what? Trying to dance to a rhythm that never quite fits?"
She nodded eagerly. "Exactly. 'Aamām'." I responded back "See? I'm not so 'pavam'."

The laughter between us softened into something gentler. She glanced again at the image of the moonlit beach. "J says the moon has two faces. One it shows the world, and one it keeps hidden. When he left for South Africa... it felt like someone flipped me to the dark side.

Everyone sees this," she gestured to her confident exterior, "but inside? Dim. And... tired."
Her voice tightened. "I just want to finish this PhD. Move on. Settle. Give time to what J and I built." She twisted her nose ring absently. "This waiting, this balancing act... it's exhausting."
I reached for her hand again, grounding us both. "You'll get there," I said quietly. "One step at a time."
She took another sip of tea, the silence stretching comfortably. "Do you think the moon ever gets tired of only showing half of itself?" she asked, almost to herself.

First journaled on August 19, 2024

♪ *Antha vaanam naan parka vendum*
A cover too similar, a flicker of dread,
Hands that twist silver rings, nerves unsaid.
Steam swirls from the cup, a ritual, a pause,
Between cheese toast bites, we redefine flaws.
"Coffee's for the edge," I whisper, light tease,
"Tea's for the moments you need to breathe."
A reluctant smile, a sip, a soft sigh,
In this fleeting calm, we let burdens lie.
The moon in her gaze, a framed picture speaks,
Super Blue Moon stretched 'cross ocean peaks.
"Rare and elusive," her voice trails thin,
"Sometimes it's hard to hold what's within."

I speak of moons, how seasons bend,
Of monthly and rare cycles that blend.
Blue not in color, but moments in time,
Fleeting and precious, a rhythm, a rhyme.
"Cherish the rare," I say with care,
"Distance and waiting—fragile to bear."
By 2027, she hopes, eyes tight,
A promise to end long hours of night.
"Do you think it tires?" she asks with a glance,
"The moon, hiding half in a wistful dance."
I hold her hand, the warmth shared deep,
"Even phases shift, even darkness sleeps."
Tamil words on music's breath,
Ease of language, the struggle with depth.
She laughs at rhythms that miss the mark,
Yet finds solace in a soft glowing spark.
The moon hides faces, one bright, one dim,
She longs for light when shadows brim.
"I just want this waiting to end,"
She whispers to stars that won't yet bend.
"To rare moments," our cups lift high,
Beneath unseen moons in silent sky.
Hope stirs in spaces where doubt has grown,
Once in a Blue Moon, she won't walk alone.
♪ *Dil mera khoya Jahaan*
♪ *Dil mera soya Wahaan*

Mayank: The next time Blue Moon appears in our sky on May 31st, 2026, Dr. Anjali will be happily married and settled.

Gunther: The three lines of Tamil in the background song are- 'Whatever you want to tell me, you can tell and go' , 'I want to revolve around the universe', and 'I want to see the skies'

19. The One with the Blood Moon

♪ **Aarambh** (Hai Prachand)- Piyush Mishra (Movie: Gulaal)

Rahul's creative journey has always been coloured by red—the kind that stains and refuses to wash away. When he began, it was about the art, the passion, the love of telling stories. It was bubblegum scripts, earrings of laughter, and lipstick marks left on crumpled screenplays, kissed with dreams. Back then, the camera captured hope and ambition—the easy allure of storytelling, unburdened by truth's harsh glare.

But time changes the shade of red. Now, Rahul sees it in saffron streets too bright to ignore, in headlines that burn, in conversations too heated to be silenced. His art has become more than escapism—it's a mirror to reflect injustice, a lens that burns with the weight of suffering. When he points his camera, he no longer seeks love; he searches for the truth buried beneath layers of indifference.

"Red matters," Rahul whispers to himself in the dark

room, surrounded by reels of film and notes that bleed frustration. He recalls directing scenes that tore open old wounds—his, theirs, everyone's. Stories of injustice, the red that stains fingers and lives. The red of sacrifice. The red of anger, burning with a flame that refuses to be snuffed out.

Look outside the windows. Look inside the huts.

The red of his film isn't just cinematic; it's real. He's met people who live with scars, who breathe in pain and exhale defiance. His stories aren't for applause anymore; they're for the cries that go unheard, the rage that simmers beneath a calm exterior. He films people's truths, knowing each frame carries the weight of a thousand silenced voices.

Red flows in silence, amidst joy and pain.

Rahul finds himself pacing during late-night shoots, questioning whether his work makes a difference. He captures red not as a romantic flourish but as a reminder—a bold, relentless push against injustice. He debates with his team, throws out scenes that feel too safe, demands they dig deeper. The red in his art has become the scream of the oppressed, the rebellion against conformity.

In every corner, in every part,
Red is the color of the human heart.

Underneath the blood moon's gaze, Rahul sits, exhausted yet defiant. The film is nearing completion, but the journey has left him frayed. He thinks of Mayank's healing, Anjali's longing, Zubin's restless soul—all pieces of a fractured world trying to find meaning. They carry their own reds—their own wounds and scars—yet here they stand, burning in different hues of the same flame.

For justice, for peace, for voices loud,
For breaking free from the conformist crowd.

Rahul's red isn't just the backdrop of his films; it's the fire that keeps him going, even when the world tells him to stop. It's the conversations that stir something deep within. The arguments, the tears, the unyielding passion that drives him forward.
And as he watches the reels spin, capturing moments of revolt, of love found and lost, of truths laid bare, he knows the red within him is not just a scream—it's the promise that stories can ignite change. Beneath the blood moon, Rahul closes his eyes, feeling the fire burn, knowing it won't be extinguished. Red is his rebellion. Red is his truth. Red is what keeps him alive.

First Penned on November 8, 2022, on a Beaver Blood Moon night

Bubblegum, Earrings, Lipstick—
The last time I wrote, it was about love.
Last time, I was naive.
Now I see saturated, visually shocking saffron,
Too bright, it blinds the eyes.
It irritates my iris, displeases my soul,
More than the romanticized emotions,
More than those red words.
The last time I wrote, it was about love,
I try to convince myself that I have evolved.
Red matters.
The broken and shattered hearts,
Just a veil to hide in our comfort sphere.
Seek the red,
Find the red.
Look outside the windows,
Look inside the huts.
Look behind the mosque,
Look behind the church.
Look at his toes, look at her arms,
And son, we will find the color we were running from:
Red.
Not crimson, nor Prussian, nor crayon,

You will find bloody red.
Red of the anger, the bloodshed, the strife,
The deep-seated pain in the fabric of life.
The red of injustice, of wounds unhealed,
The truths that our society often conceals.
From the bright saffron streets to the shadowed lanes,
Red is the pulse that courses through our veins.
In the temples, in the streets, in the sacred and profane,
Red flows in silence, amidst joy and pain.
The color of revolt, of cries unheard,
The hue of the fight, of broken words.
Red is the ink that writes our plight,
The stark reminder of the perpetual fight.
Red in the flags of nations torn,
In the eyes of the weary, the hope reborn.
It's the heart of the matter, the core of the truth,
The color of rebellion, the fire of youth.
So when we look, truly see,
Red is the essence of our plea.
For justice, for peace, for voices loud,
For breaking free from the conformist crowd.
This red is not just a shade but a scream,
For a society more just, more redeemed.
The last time I wrote, it was about love,
Now I write of red, the push, the shove.
The stark reality, the bold, the brave,
The red that courses, the red that saves.

In every corner, in every part,
Red is the metaphorical colour of the human heart
लाल मानव हृदय का रूपकात्मक रंग है
ചുവപ്പ് മനുഷ്യ ഹൃദയത്തിന്റെ രൂപക പ്രതീകമാണ്
ಕೆಂಪು ಮಾನವ ಹೃದಯದ ರೂಪಕಾತ್ಮಕ ಬಣ್ಣವಾಗಿದೆ
ਲਾਲ ਮਨੁੱਖੀ ਦਿਲ ਦਾ ਰੂਪਕਾਤਮਕ ਰੰਗ ਹੈ
लाले मनुष क दिल के प्रतीकात्मक रंग ह
লাল মানব হৃদয়ের রূপক রঙ
Woof-woof (sniffing sounds) grr (tail thump) whine (happy panting) woof! (symbolic expression of depth and connection)

Mayank: The next time Red Moon appears in our sky on March 14, 2025, Rahul's film 'Fiction' would probably be complete, deciding on its distribution channels, but Red would till be left and comodified by the genre called Romance. And Rahul would still have these thoughts.

Gunther: Blood moon is a total lunar eclipse which occurs when the Earth, Sun, and Moon align so that the Moon passes into Earth's shadow. During a total lunar eclipse, the Moon turns a reddish hue because it's within the darkest part of Earth's shadow, called the Umbra.

20. The One with the Black Moon (The Dark Side)

♪ **Moon**- Kid Francescoli

Zubin's **Sony ICD-PX470** *was lying on the desk, with a visible date stamp,* **31/12/24***. Rachel entered the room swiftly, scanning through the items on the floor.*
[Ambient Sounds]

The terrace of Dhathathreya House was alive with laughter, music, and the glow of string lights. Rahul's boisterous laughter mixed with Anjali's melodic voice, and Zubin's occasional witty remarks floated up with the night air. We were all up there, celebrating the close of another year, surrounded by warmth and memories. Above us, the stars sparkled against the inky sky, and glasses clinked in quiet resolutions and unspoken hopes. It was a moment that felt suspended in time—one of those rare breaths where life just paused.

But not everyone was accounted for.

Meanwhile, downstairs:
The recorder, a sleek little device with a blinking red

light, rested on the low wooden table by the window. Its soft hum was barely audible over the distant music drifting down from the terrace.

Rachel, always curious and never one to ignore a scent trail or a curious light, padded softly into the room. Her nose twitched, drawn by the faint smell of metal and the familiar scent of Zubin. Tap-tap-tap. Her nails clicked on the floor as she circled the table, sniffing the recorder. She nudged it with her nose—harder than necessary, perhaps. The blinking light turned solid, and a soft beep signalled the start of playback.

The Recorder's Playback: [Recording begins: December 31st, 2024, Zubin's voice, tired but warm]

Zubin's Voice: "December 31st, 2024. Note to self: Note to self: Letting go feels like releasing a breath you didn't even realize you were holding. A New Year's promise, wrapped in the dark embrace of this Black Moon—silent, hidden, but there. I wonder what the next turn of time will bring..."

[Sound of clinking glasses and distant laughter.]
Zubin's Voice: "The others are up on the terrace, toasting to beginnings and endings under starlight. I needed this pause—a moment to feel the stillness, just one breath in

the dark, before the noise rushes in again." **Guchipudi**
[Chuckle]
[Soft click. Recording shifts backward.]

[Recording: December 1st, 2024]
Zubin's Voice: "Rahul laughed wholeheartedly today. I hadn't heard it like that in months—full, uninhibited. It reminded me of the evenings in Manipal when everything felt simpler. His weird laugh can light a room; I'd forgotten that."

[Sound of pen scratching, wind rustling leaves.]

[Pause. Another click. Static crackles.]

[Recording: November 20th, 2024]
Zubin's Voice: "Mayank's healing, I think. Or maybe he's just gotten better at pretending. I see it when he thinks no one's looking—how his hands tremble when they're still. He's trying, though. Aren't we all?"

[Soft hum of wind. Recorder shifts again.]

[Recording: November 15th, 2024]
Zubin's Voice: "The Beaver Moon. Winter's coming. I hope we're ready for it. Hope Mayank's ready, too. Healing isn't linear. I know that. But I want to believe he

can make it through the dark."

[Click. A few seconds of silence, then another recording.]

[Recording: October 18th, 2024]
Zubin's Voice: "Rachel. She's... something. Wild, but with this uncanny ability to read the room. I've never seen a dog stare you down like she knows your secrets. It's unnerving and comforting all at once. Anjali's lucky to have her. Maybe we all are."

[Quick rewind. Static fades.]

[Recording: September 30th, 2024]
Zubin's Voice: "The temporary moon. Mini Moon, they call it. A cosmic visitor, here for a moment and then gone. It's like us, isn't it? We come together, we drift apart. Temporary orbits, temporary bonds. I don't know. Maybe I'm romanticizing it. But there's something in the way we come back, even when it's hard."

[Recording skips. Heavy rain in the Background.]

[Recording: August 2024]
Zubin's Voice: "Sometimes I wonder if I've recorded too much. If I'm clinging to moments because I'm afraid of

what comes next. What if all this disappears, and I'm left with just the silence? I guess… I'm scared of that. Of being left behind."

[Fast rewind. Multiple clicks.]

[Recording: March 2024]
Zubin's Voice: "I plan to visit Manipal by the end of this year. I will relive it all again after so long. I will meet the Three Muskeeters gang—Rahul & Mayank. It will be strange and familiar. Like slipping into an old coat that doesn't quite fit but carries your scent. I don't know what to make of it."

[Final click of the Playlist. Static, then one last recording.]

[Recording: February 2024]
Zubin's Voice: "Note to self: Don't forget why you started recording. Don't let the noise drown out the moments that matter. Do no let this Industry bring out the worst in you"

[Recorder clicks off. Static Noise]
[Recorder clicks on]

[Voices: Mayank, Rahul, Anjali, Zubin. Background

noises: clinking glasses, muted laughter, the distant hum of street sounds.]

Rahul, jokingly:

"You know what's next, right? Ice cream. No night ends properly without it."

Laughter bursts out, followed by the scraping of chairs against the floor. Zubin's chuckle cuts through, warm but tinged with weariness.

Mayank, softly, reflective:

"Is this what nothingness feels like? Not sharp like pain, not heavy like sorrow, but a quiet blur, where emotions flicker and dim out before they can ignite."

A pause. Water rushes in the background, its sound growing louder. The soft click of a mic being adjusted.

Zubin's Personal Entry, voice slightly muffled, as if recorded in a quiet room:

"Sometimes, even the loudest of us go quiet. I've seen it—when Mayank stops talking, when Anjali looks at the horizon as if searching for something she can't name. I record these moments because they remind me that even chaos has silence. And in that silence, there's a truth we can't ignore."

Rachel whines softly, her breath heavy as she moves closer. The faint shhh-crash of waves rolls in and out.

[Background noises: Waterfall sounds, footsteps crunching on pebbles, echoing voices.]

Mayank's voice, thoughtful, layered with tension:

"You know, sometimes you just have to write the words, even if they don't fit. Just let them breathe."

The sound of a chair creaking as someone shifts. Soft murmurs, the scrape of metal against ceramic.

[Background noises: Café ambience—clinking spoons, muffled conversations, the hiss of a coffee machine.]

Anjali, pensive, voice softened by distance:

"Sometimes, I feel like life pulls us into different orbits. We collide, we drift, and then..."

The sound of a pen tapping against a table. Soft sighs, the scrape of a spoon stirring a drink.

Mayank, in reply, with a hint of realization:

"It's just a word I use—each of us has our own path, our own orbit. We circle around our lives, sometimes close, sometimes far. Occasionally, we come together, but most of the time, we're pulled along by our own gravity."

A quiet nod of understanding. A brief moment of silence, broken by a distant car horn.

[Transition—faint sounds of distant waves and soft laughter.]

The sound of a train horn in the distance, growing

louder. Heavy, rhythmic thudding as it passes. Voices are barely audible over the roar, Kuuuuuuuuuu

[Background noises: Metal creaking, the soft whir of wind through gaps in a bridge's structure.]
The train passes, leaving behind a deep, resonant silence. Mayank's voice, quieter, almost lost to the wind:
"Progress isn't defined by speed or scale—it's the quiet shift, the subtle promise that things will not stay as they are."

The sound of deep, rhythmic breathing. The faint tick-tock of a clock, each second slipping by.
The camcorder clicks off, leaving behind only the soft sounds of the night and Rachel's slow, steady breaths.

[Mayank's voice, softly, reflective:]
"Is this what nothingness feels like? Not sharp like pain, not heavy like sorrow, but... a blur where feelings dim out before they catch fire."
[Pause. Water rushes. The mic clicks softly.]

Zubin's Personal Entry, voice muffled:
"Sometimes, even the loudest go quiet. I've seen it—Mayank, Anjali, even me. Silence is truth. We all hide there."

[Rachel whines softly, her breath slow. Waves shhh-crash in and out.]

[Recorder clicks off. Silence.]

Mayank: The next time Black Moon appears in our sky on May 2027, invisible to the eyes, it remains uncertain where Zubin's orbit will lead—whether he'll be a wanderer in search of moments to hold or find himself anchored, deeply rooted with those he once called home. May be Zubin would search for love, be content with his passion, with names on bigger screens, beyond Netflix. Zubin's journey is one of seeking connections while fearing their loss.

Gunther: A **Black Moon** is often considered the opposite of a Blue Moon and represents a rare astronomical event. It occurs when there are multiple New Moons (Amavasya) in a calendar month or season, or sometimes no New Moons in a calendar year. Like any other New Moon, it remains **invisible in the sky**, as its unilluminated side faces Earth while only its far side is bathed in sunlight; Sun-Moon-Earth in a line.

- The most common type is the **Monthly Black Moon**, which is the second New Moon in a single month, happening approximately every 29 months, with the next occurrence around May 2027.

• Another type is the **Seasonal Black Moon**, which is the third New Moon in a season that contains four New Moons, occurring about once every 33 months, with the next expected around August 2025

21. The One with the Mini-Moon 2024PT5

♪ **Where Is My Mind?** – Pixies

The day is 25th November. The Mini-Moon left Earth's orbit today. There will be only one Moon for Earth, from tomorrow onwards, and only one natural illuminating satellite, as per the astronomical science.

The terrace of Dhatathreya glowed softly under strings of lanterns, casting a warm, silver light that mingled with the thing crescent of silvery hue of the Moon. Tonight, everything felt heightened, every sound sharper, every laugh echoing just a little longer. It was the kind of evening that held the weight of goodbyes, even when no one wanted to say them out loud. No grand occasion, no planned event—just the gravitational pull of something deeper, drawing everyone together. Like one of those perfect, unscripted *Friends* episodes, but with their own twist.Anjali had an announcement to make.

Anjali, always the Monica of the group with her organization skills and warmth, moved through the gathering with ease. "Okay, seriously, what's going on?

No birthdays, no festivals, and here we are? I didn't even get a chance to clean up!" She feigned exasperation, but the smile on her face betrayed her excitement.

After ages, Niharika, Shruti and Fiaz were also able to take some time out, and have a good old fashioned get together. Party on Friday is an uncommon thing. But when one has to be considerate of everyone's availability, such things happen, and everyone needs to compromise.

Rahul, channeling his inner Phoebe, chimed in with a playful shrug. "Clearly, Anjali, the universe called and said, 'Bring your best humans together for an unscheduled vibe check.'" He waved his hands in a mock spiritual gesture, eliciting **laughter** from everyone.

Zubin, the group's resident Chandler with his wit and impeccable timing, added, "Or maybe the universe knew that if you didn't get to micromanage an event at least once more, you'd explode. Consider this an intervention."

Mayank joined in too, " November 25th is also the International day for the Elimination of Violence Against Women".

Anjali rolled her eyes, but her smile softened as she looked at everyone. "You're all ridiculous. But... now that you are all here...."

She took a deep breath and raised her glass. "I've got news."

Everyone's focus on Anjali now. "My second paper has been published. I can finally submit my thesis, and that means… I'll be leaving Manipal soon, probably early 2025."

The announcement hung in the air, filling the space between the strings of lanterns and the moonlight with a bittersweet tension. Mayank felt a pang of pride mixed with an ache he couldn't quite shake. He was proud of her, of everything she'd accomplished, but she had become one of the closest friends he'd ever had in Manipal.

Niharika—embodying the compassionate essence of Erica—reached over and squeezed Anjali's hand. "Anyway, that's incredible, Anjali. The world's going to be lucky to have you out there ." Although her first reaction was gloomy—"What is this, Ma ? You are leaving? This is toh new information only!"

Shruti, channeling David the Scientist Guy, adjusted her glasses thoughtfully. "I'm going to miss your meticulous event planning. But you know what? This is just another phase shift, like changing states of matter—solid friendships into fluid distances."

Anjali laughed, a mix of relief and sadness in her eyes. "Thanks, you guys. Really."

Zubin clinked his glass against Mayank's. "Looks like we're all on the move soon. Thrissur for Rahul. Mumbai for my 'filmy struggles,' as you so lovingly put it."

Rahul raised his glass too, the philosophical Phoebe of the group finding a serious note. "Change is inevitable. Even our little orbits have to shift."

The conversation dipped and weaved through shared memories and plans, touched with the underlying knowledge that this chapter of their lives was coming to an end. They were each headed in different directions, like the temporary moon leaving Earth's orbit.

Faiz—always the witty and grounded Mike of the group—piped up from the side. "Can we at least make a pact to not be those friends who say, 'Let's meet again soon!' and then never actually do?"

Anjali laughed with Faiz, toasted with Niharika, and

leaned into conversations with a warmth that was uniquely hers. But every so often, her eyes would drift—finding Mayank, as if to anchor herself, as if to remind them both that this was real. A journey that both of them started together, but one made it to the finish line.

As the laughter began to settle, and glasses were raised in a silent toast to memories and unspoken emotions, Rahul, always one to spark an unexpected twist, tapped on his phone. “Alright, everyone. Before we sink any deeper into nostalgia, I’ve got a little surprise.”

He held up his phone, the screen flickering to life. Moments later, Prajwal’s familiar face appeared from New York, bright sunlight streaming through the windows behind him. “Hey, you lot! I couldn’t miss this, even if it’s barely noon here,” he said, shading his eyes dramatically from the midday glare. “Why is it that every time you all gather, I feel like I’m back in a college hostel room?”

The group erupted into cheers. “Prajwal!” Anjali’s voice was bright, though it wavered with emotion. “You’re really here!”

“Virtually, yes,” Prajwal replied, tilting his camera slightly to show a typical bustling day in New York. “No fancy evening for me—just coffee breaks and work, but you all know how to bring me back, even from thousands of miles away."

"Can't resist, can we?" Zubin teased with a laugh. "It wouldn't be a proper gathering without roping you in, no matter what time zone you're in."

Before anyone else could add a comment, another face appeared on the call—Abhinav, looking slightly flustered but unmistakably delighted. "Hey, everyone! I've got maybe five minutes before rehearsal starts, but I had to check in."

"Abhinav!" Mayank called, smiling wide. "Still a man on a mission?"

"You bet," Abhinav replied, his words punctuated by the noise of a busy theatre set behind him, with a group wearing skulls as costumes humming- "आन, बान, शान या कि जान का हो दान, आज एक धनुष के बाण पे उतार ....". Trying to overpower the background noise, Abhinav said, "Actors to pep up, sets to tweak, and a performance waiting. But this? Worth every second. Anjali, you're making history."

"Thank you, Abhinav," Anjali said, her voice soft, her

gratitude evident. "It means a lot."

Finally, after a slight delay, another familiar face joined—Shetty Brother, the hum of a studio bustling in the background. "Am I late?" he asked, a teasing glint in his eye. "I might be between meetings. Something to do with a small name—Shah Rukh Khan, maybe?"

The group erupted into groans and laughter. "Trust you to drop SRK into casual conversation!" Zubin exclaimed, shaking his head.

Mayank being a fanboy asked, "Where are you now ?" "Mannat, baby !!"Shetty Brother grinned, then his expression turned briefly serious. "But really, Anjali—congratulations. You deserve this moment."

While others were still perplexed about his call from Mannat, Anjali smiled, focusing on the second line, her eyes shimmering. "Thanks, Shetty. Thank you, all of you." She looked at Rahul, acknowledging his effort to assemble the group. The thing that Dr. Richard used to do.

"Alright, enough with the mushiness," Zubin interrupted, his voice light but thick with meaning. "Before I actually start bawling."

“Agreed,” Rahul said, lifting his glass again. “A toast—to friends who became family. To every path that diverges and leads us back.”

The glasses clinked once more, the soft glow of the lanterns and the silver crescent moon illuminating their gathering. The voices from the video calls blended seamlessly into the moment, carrying warmth, joy, and the bittersweet understanding that change was inevitable, but connection was everything. Somewhere in between we ended up saying, “To Richard.” A mutual loss for all of us.

"Okay, chalo milte hain. Tata, I gotta go!" Abhinav left the call.
"Me too, Macha! Love you all. " So did Shetty Brother.

Prajwal spoke up once more, “Promise me, next time, we do this in person. No screens.”

“No excuses,” Faiz added, grinning at the camera and looking down at Rachel- tongue hanging out her mouth. “And Rachel will still be louder than all of us.”

Woof. Woof. Rachel bounded into the midst of it all—her nails clicking on the stone tiles of the terrace, tail wagging furiously. She made her way to Niharika, who had been nursing a glass of vintage wine she'd proudly brought. Rachel's keen nose twitched as she sniffed the air, clearly intrigued by the unfamiliar scent.

Niharika's eyes widened as Rachel edged closer, sniffing with more intent. "No, no, no, Rachel!" Niharika said, her voice rising in alarm. She tried to step back, but Rachel was persistent, her interest fully piqued.

"Easy, Rachel! This is vintage!" Niharika exclaimed, half-laughing, half-scolding, as she lifted her glass higher, out of reach. Rachel barked in response, her tail thumping against the floor in what could only be described as an enthusiastic attempt to say, *I want to understand this too!*

The scene broke whatever solemn air had lingered, drawing laughter from everyone else. Zubin leaned over with a teasing grin. "Rachel has impeccable taste, Niharika. You should feel honored."

"Oh, I feel *something*," Niharika muttered, taking another cautious step back while Rachel's gaze stayed fixed, ears perked and tongue lolling. "Mostly fear of losing this very expensive glass."

The laughter rippled across the terrace, breaking the tension and drawing them back together in a shared, light-hearted moment. It was Rachel, as always, weaving her way into their lives, adding chaos, warmth, and a dash of unpredictability.

The night stretched on, yet it felt like time had slowed, holding every moment between breaths. The terrace was a swirl of laughter and gentle murmurs, lanterns flickering like fallen stars in the soft breeze. The silvery crescent moon hung low, casting its light on the familiar contours of Dhatathreya, illuminating faces that would soon be seen less often. Beyond the edge of the terrace, Angel's Court stood, dark and quiet—a shadowed reminder of everything that had been and all that was yet to come.

Anjali found Mayank leaning against the boundary wall, his gaze fixed on the distant silhouette of Angel's Court. He seemed lost in thought, the lines of his face softened by the glow of the lanterns decorated by her on Diwali. She approached slowly, her footsteps light but purposeful. For a moment, she simply stood beside him, silent, letting the chill of the evening seep into their quiet understanding.

"Still looks the same," she said, nodding toward Angel's

Court. Her voice was soft, carrying the weight of familiarity and the sharp edge of change.

Mayank smiled faintly but didn't take his eyes off the house. "It's stubborn that way," he replied. "Some things don't change, even when everything else does."

They fell into silence again, the kind of silence that speaks more than words. The moon hung heavy above them, its pale light tracing the edges of their lives, their memories. Anjali leaned forward, elbows on the railing, her eyes on the moon's reflection shimmering in a puddle below. "I need to ask you something," she said, her voice careful, as if afraid of shattering the fragile moment.

Mayank turned to her, sensing the seriousness in her tone. "Anything."

Anjali exhaled slowly. "I need you to stay here, at Dhatathreya. After I leave." She paused, her words catching in her throat. "I can't bear the thought of it being empty. It deserves more than that. It deserves someone who understands what it meant to all of us."

The weight of her request settled around them. Mayank's throat tightened, and he looked away, back at Angel's

Court, as if seeking comfort in its familiar darkness. "I always thought... I'd be staying there. At Angel's Court. Watching from a distance." He swallowed hard. "But I get it. Dhatathreya is... different."

"It is," Anjali agreed, her voice barely above a whisper. "It's a house of beginnings and ends. Of laughter and pain and every messy moment in between. I want it to keep living, even if I'm not here to see it."

Mayank nodded slowly, the light catching the glimmer of unshed tears in his eyes. "I'll do it," he said, his voice rough. "But you have to send Rachel over. She's the only one who can boss me around and get away with it."

Anjali's laugh was soft, like the rustle of leaves in a gentle wind. "Of course. She'll come running, paws skidding, barking at the moon. You know how she is."

They stood in silence once more, the crescent moon above them a thin line between darkness and light. It seemed fitting—a reminder that even as the night consumed more of its glow, it would always wax again, brightening in its own time. Just like their lives, shifting through phases of presence and absence, loss and connection.

Anjali touched his arm, her fingers light, but the gesture heavy with meaning. "You'll be okay," she whispered. "You always find a way."

"Maybe," Mayank replied, his voice breaking slightly. "But it won't be the same."

"No," Anjali agreed, her eyes shimmering with unshed tears. "It won't. But you'll keep it alive. You always do."

He wanted to believe her. He wanted to hold onto this moment and never let it end. But time pressed on, like the Mini Moon, always moving, always changing.The wind picked up, rustling the lanterns, sending their light dancing across the terrace. In that moment, it felt like even the moon bowed in acknowledgment—of endings, of beginnings, and of everything that hangs delicately in between.

Mayank opened his phone,
"Beach tomorrow?" he typed into their group chat, not really expecting a reply. But it wasn't about getting a response—it was about showing up, about honoring the moments they had left.
The wind picked up, lifting a few scattered pages and sending them fluttering across the terrace. Mayank exhaled, feeling the ache and the promise of what lay

ahead. He wasn't ready. But maybe, just maybe, he didn't have to be.

A Brief Orbit: Earth's Temporary "Mini Moon" 2024 PT5 Makes Its Return

By Prajwal Manipal | Columbia Journalism Review

From September 29 to November 25, 2024, Earth hosted a rare cosmic visitor: 2024 PT5, informally known as the "Mini Moon." Unlike our permanent lunar companion, this small asteroid was temporarily captured by Earth's gravity, providing a fleeting but fascinating sight for astronomers and stargazers. "Temporary moons like this allow us to study near-Earth objects in unique ways," said Dr. Luara Spence of the Mionr Planet Centre. "They remind us of the dynamism and unpredictability of our cosmic neighbourhood."

While no threat to Earth, 2024 PT5's brief capture underscores important dynamics in gravitational interactions and orbital mechanics. Researchers have traced its movements and expect its return in 2055. Dr. Awanr Sethi, an astrophysicist at the Indian Scape Research Organisation, remarked, "These rare visitors expand our understanding of orbital dynamics and serve as living laboratories for planetary defence strategies."

For scientists and enthusiasts alike, such temporary moons highlight the intricate dance of celestial objects around Earth and our place within a dynamic universe.

Mayank: The next time the Mini-Moon appears in our orbit in Two Thousand Fifty-Five, we five will be old. And, if we're facing the bitter truth—Rachel will no longer be with us.

Zubin, with silvered hair, would either be a celebrated maverick director or still passionately critiquing an unyielding industry, his sharp wit as biting as ever. Rahul would likely be a wise figure in Thrissur, surrounded by books, seekers, and stories, his once-boisterous laughter now mellow but retaining its spark. Anjali would have realized her dream of a vast dog shelter home, each day spent nurturing countless tails and fostering hope with her unwavering kindness.

As for me? I would find myself somewhere quiet, looking up at the rare moon, feeling each wrinkle and every memory etched into my soul, if not dead.

PS: Read the starting line of this chapter again.

16. A Full Circle—Shade No. Sixteen

♪ **Raat Pohale** – Ishan Mitra (Movie: Dracula Sir)

Memory held fragments, scattered and frayed,
All the broken echoes from paths I strayed.
Yielding to shadows, I carved out another,
A name for my fear—my twin, my brother.

Night wrapped itself in every piece of me,
Knitting together masks no one could see.
In twilight's shroud, we trace paths anew,
Soft echoes of journeys that once we knew.

Luminous beams dance in this Cold Moon's breath,
Underneath frigid stars, I ponder life and death.
Never fully broken, pieces rise to mend,
A resilient light bending through phases to ascend.

Rising echoes whisper beneath the cold night,
& (And) within their embrace, I seek new light.

Lulled by shifting phases, striving to mend,
Unwavering truths through the cold extend.
Night bows softly as darkness takes flight,
Answers revealed in winter's quiet light.

Rising echoes of memories long concealed,
In the bond of F.R.I.E.N.D.S, every facet revealed.
Splitting through dark, on December Fifteen
Mr. A's reflections linger where truths convene.
Embrace the reality, of this Shade number Sixteen.

Category: This is an Acrostic Poem
An acrostic poem? Take a moment to look it up. Familiarize yourself with it, absorb the idea. I'll be right here, patiently waiting for you.

Please read the following. Once you grasp the message I'm trying to convey, you'll understand.

Dear You,

Yes! You, the one reading this now, whether it's in your hands, glowing on a screen, or worn from use. I have a final message.

The hoodie with the logo of a bat-in-a-yellow-circle lies draped over the chair, an unfinished script waits on my desk, and a cup of lukewarm carrot juice sits close by—

small details in a life lived like fragments in silent orbit. Over the years, I became a voice for every doubt, every tempest that roared inside. I was once the broken Mayank—the one who wept alone, who wandered aimlessly, wrapping himself in shadows for comfort.

They called me Mayank, and every struggle I faced became a reflection, a shade I could not ignore; shades of Lunar. In time, truth arrived—not with force, but gently, settling where the shadows used to linger. I spent too long dividing my burdens, pretending someone else was carrying what was mine to bear. But every ache, every glimmer of hope that felt so distant—it was always me. I carried it, I shouldered it alone.

The words we shared were genuine. I still ask myself if they touched the air, if they held the same weight for you as they did for me. Memories have a way of blurring, of becoming something different when the truth feels too sharp. They become stories we're willing to tell ourselves, threads we use to patch the gaps in our being.

In the end, we are nothing but the stories we keep. And, in this story, there were few also few friends, and their facets.

The moon doesn't need to stay full to shine. Neither do I.

Now that the veil is lifted, perhaps our paths may never cross again. Thank you for staying until the end. Farewell, my friend.

Yours Truly,
Mayank Agarwal
Mayank R. Agarwal
M. R. A.
Mr. A

—

Through the sounds of mortifying breaths—inhale, exhale—the crushing waves—shhh-crash, shhh-crash, scattered papers fluttered—crinkle & rustle—Mac D wrapper crumpled underfoot, the metallic clink of the key to the room in Manipal Residency—a familiar sound —gurudwara chant in the distance—calming. Clicking of keyboards—tap-tap-tap—words form a question in Osho melody; ink from the tip of the pen oozed—drip, blot— onto a crumpled napkin, a rant on not finding a pen. Supercollisions of moon and secrets—crash & reverberate. Chirp of crickets—chirp-chirp—rustle of leaves. Chai being sipped—slurp. Ice cubes dropped in a glass—clink-clink. Tattarrattat—a knock. An email chime

—ding........
Through the bulge of sea swelled and receded—the blame of gravity pulling and releasing.....
Through an wolf-like howl—
Woouuuuuuuuuuuuuuuuu.....
Through an open & upbeat machine voice; Three Tamil lines whispered like a secret; A raging red—flash, burn; Recorder's clicks—click-click-click,
And through the Laughter of FRIENDS—ha-ha-ha, we have come a full circle, in that exact specific order. If you do not believe, go ahead—flip the pages, start again. This time, listen; **DO NOT** just **READ**.

THE CYCLE BEGINS

I feel like everything has hit a reset button—my academic aspirations are gone, and the world feels weightless but eerily empty.

S.O.L: The Prequel

20 Shades of Love

Anogh Roy Acharya

20 Shades of Love is *not* an anthology.
Some might say it is a collection of 21 poems, tracing the journey of heterosexual love through the lens of a male artist's life, as time bends and seasons change. But they would be mistaken.
This is a hand-stitched carousel of moments frozen in frames; frozen into pictures. Pictures that carry the weight of emotions—a frown etched on an unhappy face, a mouth salivating with the bittersweet taste of hope, a crumbled letter heavy with unspoken words, a tortured girl's silent plea, the geometry of a rhombus shape unbalanced yet whole, a resting face lost in thought, fingers tracing tiny moles like constellations, a crazy poet's fervor, an artist in love with their muse, tears rolling in slow surrender, a stinging slap left on a cheek, the hallucination of a moon that never existed, the silent shade of monochrome skies, white waves crashing against time, a watch stopped at 11:11, tea sipped from a wine glass, hexagonal specs framing the world

differently, pixelated promises, a full stop, and a half-blank page still waiting for its story.
Each image, vivid and raw, is presented exactly in that order.

Why? Because you, my dear reader, deserve clarity—for now. But clarity is a fickle friend. With every turn of the page, meaning will dissolve into abstraction, leaving only impressions behind. The pictures will begin to blur, the lines will curve, and you will find yourself suspended in a haze of unspoken truths.

This book is **not** meant **to be *read*** in the traditional sense. No, this is a gallery of emotions to be ***seen* and *felt***—a quiet invitation to stop searching for sense and instead surrender to the rhythm of the images. These **pictures** are not hard to interpret, if only you stop trying.
So, go ahead. Flip the pages. Let the words pull you in—not as they are, but as *you* are, deep inside. Let the poems mirror your truths, your shadows, your light.
Because love, in all its shades, isn't about finding meaning—it's about living it.

Dedication

To all the people who taught me- what is love; and what is not.

To all the people who showed me- how to love; and how to not.

To all the people who tried to love me like my parents did; Anindya & Sathi.

Moreover, To Love !

A Note of Thanks

The journey began way back; and the road ahead is way too long, but I will still walk.

I convey my regards to everyone's path that my crooked roads collided with; but more significantly to- *Those who know, they know (If not, grab a copy of the First Edition)*

20 SOL. Another Preface

Kids, I'm going to tell you an **incredible story**. The story of how I met your mother... Pfft.

Relax, this isn't the year **2030** (at least not at the time of writing), and I am definitely not **Theodore Evelyn Mosby**, a.k.a. **Ted**.

I'm **Mayank—Mayank Agarwal**. I hail from a **student town** called **Manipal**, nestled along the **southern coasts of Karnataka**. The following pages hold a **story** divided into **21 parts**—or maybe just **20**, depending on how you choose to see it. And yes, I'll be in it.

I am the **co-protagonist**, alongside **Sindhu**. Ah, **Sindhu**—what a **beautiful name**, isn't it? Funny thing, though: her name literally means **sea** or **ocean** (originally), yet she had never seen the **sea**—or even set foot on a **beach**—until she met me. I first encountered **Sindhu** on a **train**, as she was **running from her past** in **Udaipur, Tripura**.

For those of you who are a bit shaky on **geography**: no, that was not a typo. I didn't mean **Rajasthan**—just like I didn't mean **Sikkim Manipal** when I said **Manipal**.

Udaipur, formerly known as **Rangamati**, is a town in the **northeastern state of Tripura**. Once the capital of the **Manikya Dynasty**, its history hums with tales of **royalty**

and **resilience**.
But perhaps I'm saying too much already. Let's leave the **storytelling** to **Mr. A**, shall we? You see, I have no idea what **A** has done with **my story**—or how **honest** he's been with the details. The **moles** on her face? The **shape** of her **spectacles**? Who knows how he's chosen to describe them? Whatever the case, he has indeed written about us—the story of an **artist** (*that's me, Mayank*) and a **poet** (*that's Sindhu*).

Now, **Sindhu** is unquestionably a **poet**, her mastery of **words** evident in every syllable she breathes. But as for me? I like calling myself an **artist**, although the more accurate term might be *mediocre sketchist*. Still, that doesn't sound nearly as **cool**, does it? **Ego-boosting** aside, **Sindhu** has inspired me in ways I never expected. I've even started **expressing myself** a little more lately.

So, in the pages that follow, sometimes you'll hear from **me directly**, and other times, **Mr. A** will do the **talking**—interpreting our **story** as he sees fit. But before I get carried away and start **badmouthing my creator**, let me remind myself of one unsettling truth:

I am **just a character**.
Or... am I?

Shade 1 (Grey Thought).

Hey You !

Hey, you !
Yes, You !
Are you happy;
As you transcend your exhilaration to the world and beyond?
Stop!
Do not think, do not stutter.
Whatever it is;
Blurt.
Now that you have become a sophisticated urbane;
Fashionable yet classy,
Gourmand yet lofty,
Why does your whiff vivacity smell stygian as it wafts, grappling my skin?
Why is the vignette of your sapient story, a gloomy catharsis?
Why don't you let the continual cascading cogitations flow free?
Why can't you be content and carefree,
Like a brook bouncing out of the earth's brink?

If this is stifling your cognitive process already, pardon my verbose verse.

What I seek to ask is simple.

Aaj khush to bahut hoge tum;
You have everything that you had desired.

But, why do you still have a daunting grin??

Shade 2 (Mauve Fear)

. Once Again

I am not sad; I am afraid.
I am afraid
That they will stay,
And my arms will stretch
To be held.
Will lick the hope,
Smell the trust,
And
Expect.

Blue ticks
Promises
Wrapped boxes
Customised portrait,
Will feel good once again;
Like warm breath
On a frosty glass pane.

Years later,
Somewhere
Someday
They will be seen again;
Trying to share a cordial smile,

As closure wasn't drawn, back then.

Hold on !

Don't get me wrong
And pity me yet.

I am not sad that they left. I am scared that they will stay
And

The raw cooked hope
Will salivate my mouth

Once again.

Shade 3 (Chartreuse Hope)

. Amma's Letter

Dear Sugar,

Hey! How are you ?
Do you remember when we were young?
Fancying world tour, and having fun.
Each month, you filled that savings jar,
And I settled for a smaller car.
I used to wonder- "How can we ever afford ?"
Expenses for two, would be too much abroad.
I thought I will ask you someday,
But then, suddenly, you passed away.

Today, I broke that jar
On the 60th anniversary, of us.
Now it has enough for one,
So let us travel the world and have fun.

Huh!
I wish you were here though,
To watch our grandson grow;
Confused, yet caring
Scared, yet loving.

Hope, one day he finds it too,
What I found in you.

His sugar,
Someday, somewhere.

Honey, I am glad;
That you have had happened.
It was a life well spent.

With Love,
Yours Forever.

4. Undyed Search

. A girl somewhere

There's a girl somewhere;
Whose shoulders are strapped,
Duties are mapped,
Arms are bent,
And tied to an invincible invisible chain.

Lines of burden
Weaving an ugly impression
On her bare membrane;
As red masquerades the colour of pain.

The shackles look flimsy
And the escape is presumed easy.
But, let me tell you my dear friend,
It is not.

Yet, she will, long before the end
Split the rope, resurrect the hope
And prove, that, she, is, not his effiing bot.

She will shine, She will rise
Like a wondrous Fugging Dynamite!

5. Pastel Yellow . She; A Diamante*

..................Beauty....................
........Charming. Tempting.........
....Cuddled, Snuggled, Loved....
. Grace, Symmetry, Lewd, Filthy.
... Groped, Clasped, Choked.....
........Forceful. Abusive..............
.................A Curse......................

** Diamante aka Diamond Poetry is a style of poetry consisting of seven lines. The text forms a rhombus shape (diamond). This form was developed by Iris Tiedt in 1969.*

6. Wheatish Shade.

Passenger no. 26

Lying beside her next to next,
She was to my right and I to her left.
Peeking from the blue sleeveless jacket,
An irresistible calm and composed face.
Marks of agony, masked by an alluring symmetry,
Invisible gray-face, over the grey dress, Making her
wheatish shade, glow in its own essence.

A sleeping beauty carved with perfect imperfection,
A sight that soothed my worries and eased my tension.
I wished the stranger to stay asleep
But a suited guy, barged in
Disturbing both me and Passenger no. 26
"Mam! May I have your ticket please ?"
And just like that, I found you,
The way Amma found Dadu.

7. Amber Promise. I have few things

I have few things
I have few things to present you for a lifetime
I have the courage, to make you mine
I have innumerous hours, to take your call
I have a shoulder, for your tears to fall
I have patience, to hear all your stories
I have the will, to make new memories
I have passion, to touch your soul
I have fingers, to tickle your tiny moles
I have it all, to fill your heart
I have the eyes, to see you as an art

I have love, more than I need
I have emotions, that I want to feed
I have warmth, to sweat your body
I have a hidden side, that will make you whisper-
"Oh Naughty"

I have laughter, to brighten your days
I have words, to weave songs of praise
I have time, to sit and watch the stars align
I have dreams, where you are mine

I have arms, to hold you tight
I have whispers, to soothe you at night

I have strength, to fight all fears
I have tenderness, to kiss away your tears
I have hope, to build a life anew
I have a promise, to always be true

And if you wonder what else I can do,
I can write an anaphora for you.

I have a 'nobody' willing to be your 'somebody'

If still not convinced, I have a confession to make.
Mademoiselle, Will you be my date ?

8.

. Pink Poet

Yes, she was a poet
And, poets are strange;
A little crazy, their thoughts unchained.

They can weave their words in shades of pink,
A hue of passion, where hearts could sink.
Blush-toned musings, soft yet bold,
Fragile whispers with stories untold.

They fall for the rusty gizmo, the cornered web,
They breathe breeze and make glee go ebb.
They gaze at stars, and admire the dark,
Never go too close to them, or they will touch your heart.

They'll make you romanticise both love and pain,
Unravel your armour, leave you bare in the game.
And yet, it's funny—amidst their artful flame,
You'll find yourself—
Still sane,
But never the same.

9.. Hazel Artist

In my life, there was art—
Abstract paintings, born from a fragile heart.
In my life, reasons to survive were few,
Canvas and palette, my shields to push through.

In my life, oxygen filled broken lungs,
Like paint brushes dipped in red, symmetrically hung.

If the walls of room number nine could speak,
They'd weep their colors and tears, until peacefully asleep

.

But now, there's you,
Revealing love in its deep, layered hue.
You made me feel; you made me care,
Your smile, your dewy-eyed stare.

Now, my world is painted by your flair,
Unaware of the art you bear.
So, Ms. Poet, you are an artist too—
Creating masterpieces out of hearts,
With hazel shades, only you imbue.

10. Addiction code . #F8DE7E

I am addicted to the morning cup of tea,
With 10 spoons of her humming, dipped in sweetness.
I am addicted to the late-night texts;
Consciously welcoming, a budding mess.

I am addicted to my heart,
Being used by fate, as a toy.
I am addicted to the handful space,
Filled with momentary joy.

I am addicted to
The extra pinch of salt in my tears,
I am addicted to
The usage of my happy masks, over a dozen layers.

I am addicted to her aroma of jasmine,
To the 2 and 1/2 moles on her chin.
I am addicted to this addiction,
That's oddly serene.

I am addicted to her unfinished sentences,
Pausing like music that doesn't want to end.
I am addicted to the way her laughter curls,

Like threads of silk weaving through my world.

I am addicted to the stories she leaves unsaid,
Echoes that linger long after we've fled.
I am addicted to her silence, too—
A quiet conversation between me and the hue.

 # F8 DE 7E
Not gold, but soft, pale, and tender.
Warm like sunrise, gentle like dusk,
Her presence paints my world in hues of quiet trust.

Her memory fills my palette, my every scene,
I am addicted to her—a light golden dream.

Time Stone

It's time, but I want to stay—a little longer,
Holding you tight to my chest, yet wishing you nearer.

I know the clock demands you to leave,
But can't we defy it, even if for a reprieve?

You can't see it; you're too naïve.
This break between us might stretch into forever's
weave.

Let me savor this fleeting moment,
Hold back the lament, shield the torment.

Freeze the jiff, lock the 'now,'
When I ask for thee, then go thou.

Please! Jizz!
Can I not let you go ?
Don't leave, do not go.

To bend the hours, hold back the unknown;
My palms are missing, one unit of time stone.

Dark Sin

We broke the vow
And committed sin,
You slapped me hard
And I got mean.

The worst in us
Took the charge,
As the best in us
Lost the urge.

Absolutely still
Black as pitch
Nothing.

In the silence, echoes linger,
A weight that no hand can lift.
Eyes that once held fire
Now shadows, adrift.

The night folds us whole,
A tapestry of regret.
We stand apart,
Two halves of a debt.

What was lost cannot be named;
What remains, darkened, stained.

Purple Sky

You felt like a dent in reality,
You tasted like two sips of eternity.
The purple sky, star dusts, the giant planet
The white moon, the waves, and the Big Ben—
Never looked so good together.

I wished it would last forever.
But the only hallucination that's untrue
Is
You.

You picked your bag, and I chose pill,
Two ways to escape, two ways to feel.
The same intent, different scripts—
A shared farewell disguised as a Trip..

Trip, trip, trip—off the edge we slip.
Drip, drip, drip—tears and time unzip.
Flip, flip, flip—the world tilts and dips.
Chip, chip, chip—awake in fractured bits.

We dissolved into colors, spilled into the sky,
Purple smeared with longing, where we said goodbye.

Together & together,
From *Move In* to *Move On* (almost) forever.

Monochrome

Here it comes once again,
With chaos, fear and pain.
It appears in broad day light,
And takes away the control of mine.

The endeavor to keep my pieces together,
Goes in vain with the dusk of sober. "Set ablaze
everything inside"
Arousing Hate for the entirety in sight,
But
I grasp my senses;
Firm and tight
Shouting out to the monster inside
"I won't give up the fight"
Not this time,
Not this time.

After all,
We are all lonely in our own fantasies,
Trying to hide under the veil of laughter,
And company.

No more whining about monochromatic life,
There is a beauty, in black and white.

White Wedding

He- her poem,
She- his art.
He got smitten,
And she; moonstruck.
2,30,000 miles, afar.

He, the new lunar.
She, The Queen of saltwater.
He and She,
The moonlit Sea.

Every night
The moment in sight
She hopped
She jumped
Waves rose
Love and hope.

Every day they waited
Till sunset;
From sunrise.
He, to look at her the entire night
And she, to grow taller
And reach the height.

She made effort,
He; stone cold.
She tried to fix him, her amore
But he was set in the monochrome.

There was rhythm in her waves
And He was... well you may say, an abstractive mess.
Both yearned
Both longed
But stayed forever, a sad song.
His fate was fixed
And her waves couldn't reach.

They blamed the Moon for being inert.
But little they knew;
The sea hopped cuz she was taught,
By the Moon; And it's gravitational pull.

In some other time and dimension,
May be the value of affection
Would solve an equation,
Like a science farted human.

The pull will be stronger,
The waves will be longer,

And they will meet, they will mate,
As newly whiteley wed;
An altered fate.

11:11

What you thought, has reached my ear ;
Message delivered, crisp and clear.
Don't ask me how,
Just know that it has, somehow.

Just so you know !
I thought of you too
Standing bare feet on evening dew
With shattered heart
And Coffee mug.

Ahh!
I wish I could lie,
I wish I knew how.
Tea is still my type;
Was then, is now.

Black tea in wine glass,
Your back, my canvas;
Paint plunged, bare fingers and skin,
Fondling, Touching, crafting skill.

My musings were understood
In spite of staying unsaid,

My nights were blue,
Days were red.
And, I will write

About those times,
As metrical composition of verselet
Like words oozing out of poet.

Yes, some words were mean,
But, we didn't mean.
Complains were stated,
Opinions were slated,
Days were dated,
Each other; hated.

Tattoos got lasered
Emotions got tampered
Heart got hurt
But

Let gone be gone
What's done is done
What's said, been said
Let it go
Come sit
Calm Down
And start again.

Hold me tight,
Wrap me around
Breathe, Whoosh!

Silence of your sound.
Hold like you don't know
'How to let go ?'
Let's start again,
For the promises made

At Eleven Eleven.

17.. A Shade called Sonnet*

Another poem? Seems boring eh?
So let's have a sonnet, instead.

1. The artist, the poet; poem and art
2. The moon and sea waves; white, black, blue and red
3. Back together all again; rewind, restart
4. Now dreams will be big, consciously made .
5. Into Love two point O; a deeper dive,
6. Chemical compositions inside head.
7. Dreaming of growing old and having child.
8. One girl for him, one dog for her; spaniel. 9. Weekend
family meetings and fine dine,
Reading books, holding hands, living, loving.
Movie nights, spending time, partner in crime,
12. Saving instagram reels; wanderlusting.
13. There is someone for everyone, if you are you
14. If still not found, wait, someone's searching too.
15.
16.

* A sonnet is a fourteen-line poem that uses one of several rhyme schemes and is composed in the metre of iambic pentameter.13th-century poet Giacomo da Lentini is credited for it. In 16th century , Sir Thomas Wyatt

introduced (Petrarchan) sonnet to England. Later, in 17th century Shakespearean or English sonnet became popular following the rhyme scheme of ABAB CDCD EFEF GG. Oh, 'why am I explaining?', you may ask. It is so, because, at times, medium is the message, and that choice itself is a task.

Etymology: Sonetto(Italian), meaning "a little sound or song."

Shade 18. . I know what love looks like

I first found love amidst an assembly crowd In a blue white school uniform amongst chattering sound
I knew exactly what it looked like
Love was chubby
Love was dusky
Love had dark brown eyes
Love made my heart beat louder
And made time move slower
But love left, due to her changing dopamine That's how my heart broke for the first time.

Love appeared in college again
World stood still. Reality didn't seem sane Love was short and skinny this time
Love looked amazing, smelled alluring But Love, chose not to be mine.

Few Years later, Love reappeared infront of my sight
At the parting moments of my farewell night. Down with six glasses of Italian cocktail, Love looked pretty with her high raised ponytail. Love wore short Kurti, and had a crooked white tooth,

Love wore small black bindi, and an anklet on one foot.
Love poured her heart and asked me for a chance,
Love promised me, more than all previous instance(?)
Love sent me cookies and cakes,
Love wrote letters to me on my birthdays, Love gave me betrayal and hate,
Love cheated on me and left.

Love vanished, oblivious of its pain
But love, came again;
This time as junior in my new degree. Oh God ! This Love was high on energy. Love fixed my wounds and rubbed my scars, Love looked good in saree and salwar, But Love mostly wore shirt and jeans, Love liked boiled rice with potato and beans. Love had freckles around her round black shimmering eyes,
Love liked pizza and whiskey with few cubes of ice.

I finally knew what love was like
But apparently, love didn't have much time So, Love became someone's wife.

Years later, love appeared,

Again.
Love has now changed,
Love has bangs on her forehead.

Love doesn’t excite,
Love is different this time.

Love has green-brown shades of eyes,
Love is scared of demise.
Love wears hexagon glasses,
Love puts on a white pocketed jacket.

Love has two and half moles on her chin,
Love maintains OCD level hygiene.
Love is beautiful, but yeah, normal;
Love seems very informal .
Love doesn’t stay awake all night,
Love prefers five to nine.

Love is politically never right,
Love gets cranky at times.
Love has wounds of her own,
Love emotes like that of a stone.

Love scribbles all day at her desk,
Love gives ample time to herself.
Love scratches and yawns,
Love uses unsophisticated words.

Love demands care, Love demands attention
But love also sticks by, in any situation.

Love makes me fight, love makes me write.
Love makes me fall, rise and push; to try harder next time .

Love doesn’t seem like love this time,
Love appears and reappears, every once in a while,
But love makes my existence worthwhile.
No matter how far it has reached, Love doesn't leave.

I finally know, exactly, what love feels like.

Sahde 19. . Pixelated Eternity

He stepped closer
And so did she
Her arms unfolded
And so did his.

Silence spoke
Hearts stroke

Remained Silent, lost in love
Vivid as reality
Till pixelated eternity

. . . .
. . . .
. . . .
. . . .
. . . .
. . . .
. . . .
. . . .
. . . .
. . . .

. . . .

. . . . . .

. . . . .

. . . .

. . .

. .

.

With few hiccups in between
Obviously!

Glitches and Stutters
Pauses in Streams.

PS: This is not a drill !

Shade 20. Period

Once upon a time there was a girl
And there was a boy
That's it.
Period.

But no, wait,
There has to be more
There needs to be a story that makes us read
There needs to be drama, there needs to be love
There needs to be a description about how they lived.

But sorry guys, this is it.
There's no more content for us to be entertained.
There was a girl and there was a boy.
That's it. The End.

. (Untitled)

.
.
.
.
.
.
.
.
.
.
.
.
.
.
.

What ?
What are you looking for ?
Oh! So you are a reader.
Are you looking for a poem ?
Or maybe a few words stitched together to deliver some meaning.

But what if there's nothing ?

What if it's just a clean black slate

Or rather white, in this case,
With no love, with no hate
No message, no order;
Just a pure stagnant mess.

What if there's no point behind all this ?
No intention behind this book,
Just puffs of words and emotions,
Rising up, as they float
In your imagination.

There's not even a designated rhyme scheme,
No alliteration, no metaphor, no theme,
No structure, no.....
There you go

There's not even a complete sentence
IT IS NOT SUPPOSED TO MAKE SENSE

However
If it does
You are beautifully insane
And since you have reached the end
This Piece of writing is Untitled

Because just like the Poem on this page
This Artist is also on a break .

S.O.L : The Sequel

XII Stave of Lore: Menoths

Anogh Roy Acharya

O.. The Measure of Moon

The word **"month"**—a small, everyday term we use without much thought—carries within it the weight of ancient skies. It comes to us from Old English **"mōnath"**, rooted in the Proto-Germanic **"mēnōths"**, meaning **"moon."** Before clocks ticked and calendars flipped, time was measured by the steady rhythm of the **lunar cycle.** In a world without screens, the **moon** was the eternal guide, its phases marking the passage of days. Every **29.5 days**, the moon completed its dance: new to full, waxing to waning, and back again. These cycles dictated ancient calendars—the **Babylonian**, **Hebrew**, and **Roman**. They shaped rituals, sowing seasons, and the very structure of human lives. To gaze at the moon was to watch **time unfold in the sky**, one phase at a time.

As the moon cast its silver glow, the ancient Romans gazed skyward, finding gods and meanings in its rhythm. They began to weave time into names, imbuing each month with the spirit of a deity or the weight of tradition.

March, the first month in the ancient Roman calendar, was born of **Mars**, the god of war. It heralded the start of action, the retreat of frost, and the promise of battles ahead.

In **April**, perhaps named for **aperire**, meaning **"to open,"** spring unfurled its quiet power. Buds awakened, and the earth stirred, embodying the hope of beginnings.

With **May**, the goddess **Maia** blessed the land with growth and fertility. Under her gentle hand, life stretched skyward, dreams unfurling alongside blossoms.

The fire of summer found its muse in **June**, named for **Juno**, the goddess of marriage and protection. In her honor, unions were forged, and love found its rhythm under golden skies.

Power then entered the calendar. **July**, renamed for **Julius Caesar**, immortalized the reformer of time itself. His influence burned as brightly as the summer sun.

August, named for **Augustus Caesar**, celebrated triumph and legacy. The first Roman emperor's achievements crowned this month, a testament to enduring greatness.

As summer waned, **September**, from **septem**, meaning **"seven,"** hummed with the rhythm of harvest. Though now ninth, its name spoke of its original place in the year.

October, from **octo**, meaning **"eight,"** followed. Autumn blazed in fleeting colors, offering beauty balanced by the awareness of decline.

November, rooted in **novem**, meaning **"nine,"** carried a quiet melancholy. Its days were sharp and reflective, a gentle descent into the stillness of winter.

Finally, **December**, from **decem**, meaning **"ten,"** once the year's end, now marked its culmination. Under winter's frost, dreams steadied, wounds found grace, and the year exhaled its final breath.

Yet, as civilizations expanded and sought precision, they looked beyond the moon. **SOLar calendars began to dominate.** The Romans, for instance, redefined the month to fit neatly into a solar year, trimming the moon's authority over time. **Julius Caesar's reform in 45 BCE**standardized the months we know today—28 to 31 days long, no longer bound to the moon's phases. And so, while the moon still shines, its measure was gently untethered from the way we mark our days.

But two months—**January** and **February**—entered the calendar later, their presence shifting the year's rhythm.

January, named for **Janus**, the Roman god of doors and transitions, became the first month. Janus, with his **two faces**, looks both backward and forward, embodying reflection and renewal. This month's spirit is one of contemplation, of stepping through the door into the unknown, while holding the lessons of the past.

February, drawn from **Februa**, the Roman festival of purification, offers cleansing and clarity. It washes away the remnants of the old year, preparing both earth and soul for the growth ahead.

But the moon's legacy persists. In its waxing and waning, in the cycles of tides and emotions, it reminds us of a rhythm older than memory. It whispers of time not as numbers, but as stories—of transitions and thresholds, of beginnings and ends.

As the months turn, each carrying their own tales and truths, perhaps we are still following the moon's rhythm. We rise, we fall. We wax, we wane. And like the moon, we carry within us the echoes of something timeless, something that refuses to be forgotten.

Time is not measured by clocks or calendars alone.
It is held in the **staves of lore**,
In the rhythm of the spaces between,
In the visuals we cherish,
In the stories we inherit,
And in what we choose to carry forward.

I.. La Marcha de Marte (Mars): Inspirado por Neruda

Marcha susurra, envuelta en vientos rojos de sangre,
La tierra tiembla, tímida pero expectante,
Por Marte, dios de los primeros pasos, que murmura:
"Comienza de nuevo, aunque la escarcha muerda el suelo."

Semillas, suaves y desafiantes, parten el suelo helado,
Sueños despiertan en las sombras de las nubes.
Una guerra silenciosa se libra—no con espadas,
Sino con corazones que anhelan la luz.

En marzo, el dolor se inclina como un retoño.
La alegría enreda sus dedos en la tierra.
El sol, medio oculto, presiona contra nuestra piel,
Su calor frágil, pero tenaz.

Marzo no enseña la paz, sino el valor de tropezar.
La escarcha y el suelo chocan,
Y la vida nace de su batalla.

Bajo este cielo, caminamos con Marte,

A través de campos que llevan nuestras cicatrices.
El pasado respira detrás de nosotros;
El futuro arde adelante—una llama de renovación.

Traducido por El Gunther

March whispers, cloaked in blood-red winds,
The earth trembles, shy yet waiting,
For Mars, the god of first steps, to murmur:
"Begin again, though frost bites the ground."

Seeds, soft and defiant, split the frozen soil,
Dreams awaken in the shadows of clouds.
A quiet war rages—not with swords,
But with hearts aching for light.

In March, grief bends like a sapling.
Joy curls its fingers into the earth.
The sun, half-hidden, presses against our skin,
Its warmth fragile, yet unyielding.

March teaches not peace, but the courage to stumble.
The frost and the soil clash,
And life is born of their battle.

Beneath this sky, we walk with Mars,

Through fields that carry our scars.
The past breathes behind us;
The future burns ahead—a flame of renewal.

II. . Aperire: A Shakespearean Lāre

In days of yore, ‘twas Aphrodite’s (Greek) grace,
That named the month which blooms doth oft embrace.
April, from Latin Aprillis, dost thou spring,
A name whose root, aperire, doth bring

The goddess’ hand through meadows stray,
Awaking the world from slumber’s gray.
Through softest winds her whispers weave,
And mortal hearts her art believe.

The streams do murmur, the woodlands sing,
Their voices rise to herald spring.
Each bloom dost tell of fleeting hours,
As April gifts her golden flowers.

Yet April’s veil is soft and thin,
Its beauty fades, its truths begin.
Behind the petals, wisdom hides,
And time reveals what spring betides.

For Venus’ (Roman) smile is sweet and brief,
Her laughter turns to gentle grief.
Yet even loss births life anew,

As earth renews beneath the dew.

O Venus bright, thy love is lore,
A fleeting glimpse of heaven's door.
Thy month dost teach us to prepare,
For change, for growth, thy gentle care.

Thus April fades, her tale is spun,
A hymn to life beneath the sun.
Her fleeting joy, her lessons rare,
Doth guide us all to ancient Lāre.

"On lāre lærð, swa feorran hider."
(Through learning or lores, wisdom journeys from afar to here)

III. . Maia fi asloob Rumi

Ya Maia, umm al-zahr wa al-namaa,
Tuhdi al-ard bi ajmal al-asmaa.
Tusabbihu al-riyah biki ila al-sama,
Dhikrayaki yajri mithl al-hawa,
Ya umm Utarid, malikat al-rabee' wa al-dhya.

Fi shahrek, tashtad al-arwah min ruqood,
Wa tataqwa al-ard, wa al-quloob tanqud.
Al-thawr al-ameen wa al-thunai al-raqiq,
Yarwi qisas al-hubb taht al-ufuq al-'amiq.
Taqood al-quloob ila ro'ya safia,
Wa nujoom bika tanzil ilahiya.

Allimna, ya Maia, fann al-sabr,
La sur'a wa la shara, bal bi tadbir al-amr.
Duroosuki fi dhil al-waqt tanbat,
Mithl al-fannan yujamil al-lawn wa al-khatt.
Min ismuki, al-qisas tatashabik wa tatadhakar,
Wa min al-sama wa al-ard, rahma nastadakir.

Ya Maia, taqaddami ma'a nasmat al-hawa,
Wazra'i al-amal fi makan kana fihi al-yas' yabki.
Aj'ali turuqan haythu lam takun,
Wa idfa'i al-dhwa' ila dhil al-maknun.

Tahta nujoomuki, al-thawr wa al-thunai yatahadan,
Wa al-arwah tashtafi wa al-qalb yataman.

Fi nasmat al-hawa, haqiqatuki tarfa',
Wa al-quloob tajid istiraha, wa al-alam yurfa'.
Tahta nazratiki, qisas al-hubb tatair,
Fi wasat al-ikhtibar, anta tatala' al-noor.
Ya umm Utarid, umm al-namaa wa al-farah,
Fi hugnik, al-quloob tadum bil-farah.

Bi sabr wa hubb, abadan yatayir,
Tahth hadratiki, taht al-sama al-faseeh.

Tarjama Al-Gunther
ترجمة الجنثر

O Maia, mother of bloom and growth,
Thou dost gift the earth with fairest of names.
The winds do sing thy praise to the heavens high,
Thy memory flows as the air takes flight,
O Mercury's mum, thou art the earth's delight.

In thy month, spirits awaken from slumber deep,
The soil dost strengthen, and hearts do leap.

The steadfast bull and gentle twins arise,
Their tales of strength and love beneath the skies.
Guiding hearts to visions pure and clear,
Their constellations dost ever draw us near.

Teach us, O Maia, the craft of patience fair,
Not haste, nor greed, but waiting with due care.
Thy lessons lie in time's soft embrace,
As painters find beauty in every trace.
From thy name, ancient tales dost weave,
Mercy and meaning from sky and earth receive.

O Maia, come forth with winds that softly sing,
Plant hope where despair its shadows doth cling.
Forge paths where none hath ever been,
And bringeth light to shadows long unseen.
Beneath thy stars, the bull and twins entwine,
And souls dost heal with whispers divine.

Through breezes soft, thy truths dost soar,
Hearts find refrain, their pain no more.
Under thy watch, tales of love take flight,
Amidst the trials, thou dost shine so bright.
O Mercury's mum, mother of joy profound,
In thy embrace, hearts ever unbound.

Through patience and love, eternal they fly,
Forever guided 'neath thy vast, open sky.

IV. . Juno's Pursuit of Cnāwelacu (Knowledge)

XXXII Staves (4 x 8)

O Juno, **consort of mighty Jove**,
Thy month dost stir the mind to rove.
Not in the snares of love's sweet chains,
But in realms where reason reigns.

Beneath thy heavens, bright and vast,
Ambition stirs, a ship's firm mast.
The quill doth dance, the scrolls unfold,
Where secrets of the stars are told.

The heart, unburdened, doth now aspire,
To reach the heights of wisdom's choir.
For passion's song hath lost its plea,
Replaced by learning's melody.

In hallowed halls where silence sings,
Five souls doth labor 'neath wisdom's wings.
In Manipal's streets where dreams take flight,
Their future shapes through toil's long night.

Thy hand, O Juno, gently guides,
Through stormy thoughts where truth abides.

No idle love, no fleeting woe,
But a path where brighter insights grow.

For thou art not a hearth alone,
But queen where aspirations are sown.
Thy **cnāwelacu** doth light the mind,
With treasures rare and paths refined.

The figure walks, unbound, serene,
Through corridors of thought unseen.
The call of Jove, thy lord, doth chime,
"To seek, to strive, beyond time's climb."

June fades with whispers, calm and sure,
A testament to minds mature.
O Juno, grant thy steady hand,
To all who seek, to all who stand.

V. Julius. Echoes of Eternity

XXV Staves (5 x 5)

O Julius, thy name doth ever resound,
Bearer of Caesar's glory profound.
Thy month dost blaze in triumph's hue,
With Leo's roar and Cancer's adieu,
A crown of fire where dreams abound.

Thy sun dost burn with steadfast might,
Illuming paths 'neath thy golden light.
In thy warmth, bold hearts take flight,
Through daring ventures, day and night,
Thy radiance kindles valor's rite.

In fields of gold, thy passions churn,
Fleeting joys to embers turn.
Thy fleeting days, where strife doth meet,
Forge souls anew in summer's heat,
And from thy lessons, hearts dost learn.

O Julius, thou dost teach through flame,
That time's swift march shall none reclaim.

To treasure each fleeting hour bestowed,
To tread the paths by courage sowed,
Thy wisdom lights life's sacred frame.

As shadows stretch and twilight falls,
Thy echoes linger, hallowed calls.
Thy crown departs, thy fire wanes slow,
Yet whispers bid the heart to grow,
Thy fleeting days still speak eternity.

VI. Augustus. The Crown of Fire

XXIV Staves (6x)

Hail, Augustus! Named for the Caesar divine,
Thy days dost blaze with the sun's scorching shine.
Thou art the monarch of summer's grand stage,
Cloaked in Leo's roar and Virgo's quiet sage.

The fields lie golden, their bounty revealed,
A mirror to dreams that our hearts once concealed.
The air doth shimmer with promise and sweat,
As ambitions rise 'neath the sun's fiery threat.

O fiery month, where boldness takes form,
Dreams arise, untouched by the storm.
A heart's labor beneath thy glowing reign,
Chases passion, though weighed by pain.

Virgo's hand doth softly prepare,
While Leo's pride burns hot in the air.
Thy fleeting days teach life to embrace,
Both triumph's fire and tender grace.

August, thou crown of the year's fierce delight,

A turning point marked by both fire and night.
Each path we walk is laden with cost,
Yet each shadow bears light, where none is lost.

Thus, thy golden sun and temperate breeze,
Guide us toward autumn's cooling reprieve.
Thy fleeting embrace, both burden and balm,
Marks the year's march with a dignified calm.

VII. Septem. The Harvest's Hymn

XXI Staves (7x)

From *septem*, the Roman tongue of old,
Thy name arose, steadfast and bold.
Though now thou art ninth, thy essence remains,
The seventh month, where the year sustains.

September, thou herald of autumn's grace,
Thy winds bring whispers, a softer embrace.
The sun, though fading, lingers yet near,
Casting long shadows, tender and clear.

Virgo, the maiden, with her gentle sway,
Turns golden fields to a harvest array.
As Libra ascends, her balance foretold,
Time bends gently, as new stories unfold.

In fields of gold, memories lie,
Each stalk a song, 'neath the endless sky.
The earth speaks softly, in echoes deep,
Of labors past, and promises to keep.

Thy fleeting days, a gentle reminder,

That endings and beginnings intertwine.
September hums with harmony divine.

For each harvest reaped, another seed's sown,
Through endings, beginnings are humbly shown.

VIII. Octo. The Balance of Change

XVI Staves (8x)

From *octo*, the Roman word for eight,
October stands where the year turns its gate.
Though now the tenth, thy roots remain,
A bridge of autumn, 'twixt sun and rain.

Beneath thy skies of ambered fire,
Dreams linger yet, as hopes aspire.
The scales of Libra, balanced and wise,
Guide us gently as daylight dies.

A chill descends, crisp leaves take flight,
Whispering secrets to the fading light.
The hunter's moon, bold and bright,
Marks the season's majestic rite.

Thy days are fleeting, thy moments brief.
A dance of colours, both joy and grief.
October speaks in tones profound,
A harmony of time unbound.

IX. Novem. Dreamt Descent

XIII Staves & ½ (9 x 1.5)

From *Novem*, ninth in Rome's array,
Thy name endureth, though time doth sway.
November whispers, in shadowed breath,
A fleeting hymn to autumn's death.

The air bites sharp, the frost takes hold,
Yet embers glow, their stories told.
The scorpion's sting, the archer's flight,
Mark the heavens with a chilling light.

Fallen leaves weave thy tapestry fine,
Each step doth echo a fleeting sign.
Of hearts that fade, of minds that stray,
Through fleeting time, both night and day.

In twilight's hush, thou dost us keep—
An end begun... (half-dreamed, half-sleep).

X. Decem. The Year's Quiet Refrain

X Staves (10x)

From *decem*, the month once tenth, now last,
The chill of endings, whispers of the past.

Sagittarius fires its arrow of might,
Capricorn ascends, steady in its plight.

Under frost's veil, old wounds find grace,
Dreams once fleeting now steady their pace.

A year's echo hums in the winter's cold,
Manipal's quiet streets, stories untold.

The year wanes gently, in its soft embrace,
A chapter closes, leaving its trace.

XI & XII. The Last Embrace

III Staves (1 + 2)

Time slips, fleeting as a lover's sigh.
Janus whispers promises, soft and shy,
Februa lingers, a tear in its eye.

20 | 16 | XII. S.O.L: The Epilogue

As the final chapter of **20 SOL**, **16 SOL**, and **XII SOL** rests in your hands, a realization dawns—these aren't just words smeared on pages or screens, but invitations to experience life differently. They are **a journey of the senses**, where each installment opens a new dimension of connection, a different way of feeling the world.

In **20 Shades of Love**, you walked through a gallery of vivid emotions, each poem a photograph suspended in time. It was a **visual odyssey**, where the lens of a male artist framed love, loss, and longing. Every image etched a memory—wheatish skin glowing in the train's dim light, a letter crumpled with unspoken goodbyes, a shadowed tear lingering on a lover's cheek. These poems didn't ask to be read but to be seen. You weren't merely a reader but a visitor in an exhibition of untamed love. You were asked to trace each stroke, each color, as though standing before a masterpiece in motion.

Then came **16 Shades of Lunar**, where the narrative shifted. Here, the moon became your guide, waxing and waning through the tides of emotions. It wasn't just words—it was an **auditory symphony**. Each chapter carried a recommended soundtrack, weaving music into the rhythm of the staves. This book didn't ask you to see;

it demanded that you listen. The hum of a violin, the whisper of a piano, the distant echo of waves—each sound became a vessel for the words. You were no longer flipping pages; you were tuning into the crescendos and silences of a human heart laid bare.

Finally, in **12 Staves of Lore**, the journey of time was brought into focus. It was not visual, not auditory, but something deeper—**a hymn to the soul**. Here, the months themselves became characters, speaking in ancient tongues and poetic refrains. The etymology of time unraveled, guiding you to reflect on the passage of days, the seasons of change, and the legacy of moments carried forward. Each stave was a marker of transformation—a quiet reminder that endings and beginnings are but two sides of the same coin.

The Interwoven Threads of S.O.L

Through these three collections, the essence of **S.O.L** unfolded in fragments, yet always intertwined. The **visual vividness** of 20 SOL laid the foundation. The **melodic immersion** of 16 SOL carried you deeper into the rhythm of life. And the **philosophical musings** of XII SOL offered you the wisdom of time itself.

This trilogy was never about the stories themselves. It was about the spaces in between—the breath between a note, the silence before the shutter clicks, the moment when the heart hesitates. It was about you. Your interpretation. Your memories. Your truths.

What Lies Beyond

As this epilogue closes, a new beginning lingers in its shadow. The moon will rise again, the months will cycle anew, and love will whisper once more. But this time, the lens is yours. The melody is yours. The narrative is yours to shape.

May the images of **20 SOL**, the harmonies of **16 SOL**, and the wisdom of **XII SOL** guide you. May they remind you that life is a tapestry woven with light, sound, and memory. And may they echo softly in the quiet corners of your heart, long after the final page has been turned.

A Final Whisper

To see. To hear (onomatopoeia). To live.

This is the essence of S.O.L.

Now, dear reader, it is your turn to carry the story forward. Let the colors, the sounds, and the lore breathe within you. Let your own shades unfold. And remember, in every ending, there lies the faintest spark of a beginning.

Yours Truly,

A Cursor blinking on White Space
The Typewriter Effect |

The keys clattered in a rhythmic **tap-tap-tap**, a staccato melody of thoughts taking form. **Click-clack**, the letters marched into line, each press a tiny percussion, each space a soft **thunk** of pause. **Tippity-tap**, the fingers danced across the keyboard, a symphony of creation woven with moments of silence. The backspace grumbled with a sharp **clack**, erasing missteps with firm precision, while the enter key rang out with a decisive **thud**, punctuating the chaos with resolution.

MR. A
Maynak R. Agarwal

The End

**In the symphony of chaos, every heartbeat is a verse,
every moment a stanza—unwritten yet eternal.**

Thank you, and that's my time.

Printed by Libri Plureos GmbH in Hamburg,
Germany

9 789367 390351